SUSPIRIA DE PROFUNDIS AND OTHER WRITINGS

By THOMAS DE QUINCEY

A Digireads.com Book
Digireads.com Publishing

Suspiria de Profundis and Other Writings
By Thomas de Quincey
ISBN 10: 1-4209-4055-4
ISBN 13: 978-1-4209-4055-8

Please visit *www.digireads.com*

CONTENTS

ON THE KNOCKING AT THE GATE
IN MACBETH

First published in The London Magazine, October 1823

FROM my boyish days I had always felt a great perplexity on one point in Macbeth. It was this: the knocking at the gate, which succeeds to the murder of Duncan, produced to my feelings an effect for which I never could account. The effect was, that it reflected back upon the murderer a peculiar awfulness and a depth of solemnity; yet, however obstinately I endeavoured with my understanding to comprehend this, for many years I never could see *why* it should produce such an effect.

Here I pause for one moment, to exhort the reader never to pay any attention to his understanding, when it stands in opposition to any other faculty of his mind. The mere understanding, however useful and indispensable, is the meanest faculty in the human mind, and the most to be distrusted; and yet the great majority of people trust to nothing else, which may do for ordinary life, but not for philosophical purposes. Of this out of ten thousand instances that I might produce, I will cite one. Ask of any person whatsoever, who is not previously prepared for the demand by a knowledge of the perspective, to draw in the rudest way the commonest appearance which depends upon the laws of that science; as, for instance, to represent the effect of two walls standing at right angles to each other, or the appearance of the houses on each side of a street, as seen by a person looking down the street from one extremity. Now in all cases, unless the person has happened to observe in pictures how it is that artists produce these effects, he will be utterly unable to make the smallest approximation to it. Yet why? For he has actually seen the effect every day of his life. The reason is- that he allows his understanding to overrule his eyes. His understanding, which includes no intuitive knowledge of the laws of vision, can furnish him with no reason why a line which is known and can be proved to be a horizontal line, should not *appear* a horizontal line; a line that made any angle with the perpendicular, less than a right angle, would seem to him to indicate that his houses were all tumbling down together. Accordingly, he makes the line of his houses a horizontal line, and fails, of course, to produce the effect demanded. Here, then, is one instance out of many, in which not only the understanding is allowed to overrule the eyes, but where the understanding is positively allowed to obliterate the eyes, as it were; for not only does the man believe the evidence of his understanding in opposition to that of his eyes, but (what is monstrous!) the idiot is not aware that his eyes ever gave such evidence. He does not know that he has seen (and therefore *quoad* his consciousness has *not* seen) that which he *has* seen every day of his life. But to return from this digression, my understanding could furnish no reason why the knocking at the gate in Macbeth should produce any effect, direct or reflected. In fact, my understanding said positively that it could *not* produce any effect. But I knew better; I felt that it did; and I waited and clung to the problem until further knowledge should enable me to solve it. At length, in 1812, Mr. Williams made his *début* on the stage of Ratcliffe Highway, and executed those unparalleled murders which have procured for him such a brilliant and undying reputation. On which murders, by the way, I must observe, that in one respect they have had an ill effect, by making the connoisseur in murder very fastidious in his taste, and dissatisfied by anything that has been since done in that line. All other murders look pale by the deep crimson of his; and, as an amateur once said to me in a querulous tone, 'There has been absolutely nothing *doing* since his time, or nothing that's worth speaking of.' But this is wrong; for it is unreasonable to expect all men to be great artists, and born with the genius of Mr. Williams. Now it will be remembered, that in the first of these murders (that of the Marrs), the same incident (of a knocking at the door) soon after the work of extermination was complete, did actually occur, which the genius of Shakespeare has invented; and all good judges, and the most eminent dilettanti, acknowledged the felicity of Shakespeare's suggestion, as soon as it was actually realized. Here, then, was a fresh proof that I was right in relying on my own feeling, in opposition to my understanding; and I again set myself to study the problem; at length I solved it to my own satisfaction, and my solution is this. Murder, in ordinary cases, where the sympathy is wholly directed to the case of the murdered person, is an incident of coarse and vulgar horror; and for this reason, that it flings the interest exclusively upon the natural but ignoble instinct by which we cleave to life; an instinct which, as being indispensable to the primal law of self-preservation, is the same in kind (though different in degree) amongst all living creatures: this instinct, therefore, because it annihilates all distinctions, and degrades the greatest of men to the level of 'the poor beetle that we tread on', exhibits human nature in its most abject and humiliating attitude. Such an attitude would little suit the purposes of the poet. What then must he do? He must throw the interest on the murderer. Our sympathy must be with *him* (of course I mean a sympathy of comprehension, a sympathy by which we enter into his feelings, and are made to understand them,—not a sympathy [1] of pity or approbation). In the murdered person, all strife of thought, all flux and reflux of passion and of purpose, are crushed by one overwhelming panic; the fear of instant death smites him 'with its petrific mace'. But in the murderer, such a murderer as a poet will condescend to, there must be raging some great storm of passion—jealousy, ambition, vengeance, hatred—which will create a hell within him; and into this hell we are to look. In Macbeth, for the sake of gratifying his own enormous and teeming faculty of creation, Shakespeare has introduced two murderers: and, as usual in his hands, they are remarkably discriminated: but, though in Macbeth the strife of mind is greater than in his wife, the tiger spirit not so awake, and his feelings caught chiefly by contagion from her,- yet, as both were finally involved in the guilt of murder, the murderous mind of necessity is finally to be presumed in both. This was to be expressed; and on its own account, as well as to make it a more proportionable antagonist to the unoffending nature of their victim, 'the gracious Duncan,' and adequately to expound 'the deep damnation of his taking off', this was to be expressed with peculiar energy. We were to be made to feel that the human nature, i.e. the divine nature of love and mercy, spread through the hearts of all creatures, and seldom utterly withdrawn from man—was gone, vanished, extinct, and that the fiendish nature had taken its place. And, as this effect is marvellously accomplished in the dialogues and soliloquies themselves, so it is finally consummated by the expedient under consideration; and it is to this that I now solicit the reader's attention. If the reader has ever witnessed a wife, daughter, or sister in a fainting fit, he may chance to have observed that the most affecting moment in such a spectacle is *that* in which a sigh and a stirring announce the recommencement of suspended life. Or, if the reader has ever been present in a vast metropolis, on the day when some great national idol was carried in funeral pomp to his grave, and chancing to walk near the course through which it passed, has felt powerfully in the silence and desertion of the streets, and in the stagnation of ordinary business, the deep interest which at that moment was possessing the heart of man—if all at once he should hear the death-like stillness broken up by the sound of wheels rattling away from the scene, and making known that the transitory vision was dissolved, he will be aware that at no moment was his sense of the complete suspension and pause in ordinary human concerns so full and affecting, as at that moment when the suspension ceases, and the goings-on of human life are suddenly resumed. All action in any direction is best expounded, measured, and made apprehensible, by reaction. Now apply this to the case in Macbeth. Here, as I have said, the retiring of the human heart, and the entrance of the fiendish heart was to be expressed and made sensible. Another world has stepped in; and the murderers are taken out of the region of human things, human purposes, human desires. They are transfigured: Lady Macbeth is 'unsexed;' Macbeth has forgot that he was born of woman; both are conformed to the image of devils; and the world of devils is suddenly revealed. But how shall this be conveyed and made palpable? In order that a new world may step in, this world must for a time disappear. The murderers, and the murder must be insulated- cut off by an immeasurable gulf from the ordinary tide and succession of human affairs— locked up and sequestered in some deep recess; we must be made sensible that the world of ordinary life is suddenly arrested—laid asleep—tranced—racked into a dread armistice; time must be annihilated; relation to things without abolished; and all must pass self-withdrawn into a deep syncope and suspension of earthly passion. Hence it is, that when the deed is done, when the work of darkness is perfect, then the world of darkness passes away like a pageantry in the clouds: the knocking at the gate is heard; and it makes known audibly that the reaction has commenced; the human has made its reflux upon the fiendish; the pulses of life are beginning to beat again; and the re-establishment of the goings-on of the world in which we live, first makes us profoundly sensible of the awful parenthesis that had suspended them.

[1] It seems almost ludicrous to guard and explain my use of a word, in a situation where it would naturally explain itself. But it has become necessary to do so, in consequence of the unscholarlike use of the word sympathy, at present so general, by which, instead of taking it in its proper sense, as the act of reproducing in our minds the feelings of another, whether for hatred, indignation, love, pity, or approbation, it is made a mere synonyme of the word pity; and hence, instead of saying 'sympathy *with* another, many writers adopt the monstrous barbarism of 'sympathy *for* another.

O mighty poet! Thy works are not as those of other men, simply and merely great works of art; but are also like the phenomena of nature, like the sun and the sea, the stars and the flowers; like frost and snow, rain and dew, hail-storm and thunder, which are to be studied with entire submission of our own faculties, and in the perfect faith that in them there can be no too much or too little, nothing useless or inert—but that, the farther we press in our discoveries, the more we shall see proofs of design and self-supporting arrangement where the careless eye had seen nothing but accident!

N.B. In the above specimen of psychological criticism, I have purposely omitted to notice another use of the knocking at the gate, viz. the opposition and contrast which it produces in the porter's comments to the scenes immediately preceding; because this use is tolerably obvious to all who are accustomed to reflect on what they read. A third use also, subservient to the scenical illusion, has been lately noticed by a critic in the LONDON MAGAZINE: I fully agree with him; but it did not fall in my way to insist on this.

X. Y. Z.

SUSPIRIA DE PROFUNDIS: BEING A SEQUEL TO THE CONFESSIONS OF AN ENGLISH OPIUM-EATER

INTRODUCTORY NOTICE

IN 1821, as a contribution to a periodical work,—in 1822, as a separate volume,—appeared the "Confessions of an English Opium-Eater." The object of that work was to reveal something of the grandeur which belongs *potentially* to human dreams. Whatever may be the number of those in whom this faculty of dreaming splendidly can be supposed to lurk, there are not perhaps very many in whom it is developed. He whose talk is of oxen, will probably dream of oxen; and the condition of human life, which yokes so vast a majority to a daily experience incompatible with much elevation of thought, oftentimes neutralizes the tone of grandeur in the reproductive faculty of dreaming, even for those whose minds are populous with solemn imagery. Habitually to dream magnificently, a man must have a constitutional determination to reverie. This in the first place, and even this, where it exists strongly, is too much liable to disturbance from the gathering agitation of our present English life. Already, in this year 1845, what by the procession through fifty years of mighty revolutions amongst the kingdoms of the earth, what by the continual development of vast physical agencies,—steam in all its applications, light getting under harness as a slave for man [2] , powers from heaven descending upon education and accelerations of the press, powers from hell (as it might seem, but these also celestial) coming round upon artillery and the forces of destruction,—the eye of the calmest observer is troubled; the brain is haunted as if by some jealousy of ghostly beings moving amongst us; and it becomes too evident that, unless this colossal pace of advance can be retarded (a thing not to be expected), or, which is happily more probable, can be met by counter forces of corresponding magnitude, forces in the direction of religion or profound philosophy, that shall radiate centrifugally against this storm of life so perilously centripetal towards the vortex of the merely human, left to itself, the natural tendency of so chaotic a tumult must be to evil; for some minds to lunacy, for others to a regency of fleshly torpor. How much this fierce condition of eternal hurry upon an arena too exclusively human in its interests is likely to defeat the grandeur which is latent in all men, may be seen in the ordinary effect from living too constantly in varied company. The word *dissipation*, in one of its uses, expresses that effect; the action of thought and feeling is too much dissipated and squandered. To reconcentrate them into meditative habits, a necessity is felt by all observing persons for sometimes retiring from crowds. No man ever will unfold the capacities of his own intellect who does not at least checker his life with solitude. How much solitude, so much power. Or, if not true in that rigor of expression, to this formula undoubtedly it is that the wise rule of life must approximate.

[2] Daguerreotype, &c.

Among the powers in man which suffer, by this too intense life of the *social* instincts, none suffers more than the power of dreaming. Let no man think this a trifle. The machinery for dreaming planted in the human brain was not planted for nothing. That faculty, in alliance with the mystery of darkness, is the one great tube through which man communicates with the shadowy. And the dreaming organ, in connection with the heart, the eye and the ear, compose the magnificent apparatus which forces the infinite into the chambers of a human brain, and throws dark reflections from eternities below all life upon the mirrors of the sleeping mind.

But if this faculty suffers from the decay of solitude, which is becoming a visionary idea in England, on the other hand, it is certain that some merely physical agencies can and do assist the faculty of dreaming almost preternaturally. Amongst these is intense exercise; to some extent at least, and for some persons; but beyond all others is opium, which indeed seems to possess a *specific* power in that direction; not merely for exalting the colors of dream-scenery, but for deepening its shadows; and, above all, for strengthening the sense of its fearful *realities*.

The *Opium Confessions* were written with some slight secondary purpose of exposing this specific power of opium upon the faculty of dreaming, but much more with the purpose of displaying the faculty itself; and the outline of the work travelled in this course. Supposing a reader acquainted with the true object of the Confessions as here stated, namely, the revelation of dreaming, to have put this question:—

"But how came you to dream more splendidly than others?"

The answer would have been—"Because (*praesmisses praemittendis*) I took excessive quantities of opium."

Secondly, suppose him to say, " But how came you to take opium in this excess?"

The answer to *that* would be, "Because some early events in my life had left a weakness in one organ which required (or seemed to require) that stimulant."

Then, because the opium dreams could not always have been understood without a knowledge of these events, it became necessary to relate them. Now, these two questions and answers exhibit the *law* of the work; *i.e.* the principle which determined its form, but precisely in the inverse or regressive order. The work itself opened with the narration of my early adventures. These, in the natural order of succession, led to the opium as a resource for healing their consequences; and the opium as naturally led to the dreams., But in the synthetic order of presenting the facts, what stood last in the succession of development stood first in the order of my purposes.

At the close of this little work, the reader was instructed to believe—and *truly* instructed—that I had mastered the tyranny of opium. The fact is, that *twice* I mastered it, and by efforts even more prodigious in the second of these cases than in the first. But one error I committed in both. I did not connect with the abstinence from opium, so trying to the fortitude under any circumstances, that enormity of excess which (as I have since learned) is the one sole resource for making it endurable. I overlooked, in those days, the one *sine quâ non* for making the triumph permanent. Twice I sank, twice I rose again. A third time I sank; partly from the cause mentioned (the oversight as to exercise), partly from other causes, on which it avails not now to trouble the reader. I could moralize, if I chose; and perhaps he will moralize, whether I choose it or not. But, in the mean time, neither of us is acquainted properly with the circumstances of the case: I, from natural bias of judgment, not altogether acquainted; and he (with his permission) not at all.

During this third prostration before the dark idol, and after some years, new and monstrous phenomena began slowly to arise. For a time, these were neglected as accidents, or palliated by such remedies as I knew of. But when I could no longer conceal from myself that these dreadful symptoms were moving forward forever, by a pace steadily, solemnly, and equably increasing, I endeavored, with some feeling of panic, for a third time to retrace my steps. But I had not reversed my motions for many weeks, before I became profoundly aware that this was impossible. Or, in the imagery of my dreams, which translated everything into their own language, I saw through vast avenues of gloom those towering gates of ingress which hitherto had always seemed to stand open, now at last barred against my retreat, and hung with funeral crape.

As applicable to this tremendous situation (the situation of one escaping by some refluent current from the maelstrom roaring for him in the distance, who finds suddenly that this current is but an eddy, wheeling round upon the same maelstrom), I have since remembered a striking incident in a modern novel. A lady abbess of a convent, herself suspected of Protestant leanings, and in that way already disarmed of all effectual power, finds one of her own nuns (whom she knows to be innocent) accused of an offence leading to the most terrific of punishments. The nun will be immured alive, if she is found guilty; and there is no chance that she will not, for the evidence against her is strong, unless something were made known that cannot be made known; and the judges are hostile. All follows in the order of the reader's fears. The witnesses depose; the evidence is without effectual contradiction; the conviction is declared; the judgment is delivered; nothing remains but to see execution done. At this crisis, the abbess, alarmed too late for effectual interposition, considers with herself that, according to the regular forms, there will be one single night open, during which the prisoner cannot be withdrawn from her own separate jurisdiction. This one night, therefore, she will use, at any hazard to herself, for the salvation of her friend. At midnight, when all is hushed in the convent, the lady traverses the passages which lead to the cells of prisoners. She bears a master-key under her professional habit. As this will open every door in every corridor, already, by anticipation, she feels the luxury of holding her emancipated friend within her arms. Suddenly she has reached the door; she descries a dusky object; she raises her lamp, and, ranged within the recess of the entrance, she beholds the funeral banner of the holy office, and the black robes of its inexorable officials.

I apprehend that, in a situation such as this, supposing it a real one, the lady abbess would not start, would not show any marks externally of consternation or horror. The case was beyond *that*. The sentiment which attends the sudden revelation that *all is lost!* silently is gathered up into the heart; it is too deep for gestures or for words; and no part of it passes to the outside. Were the ruin conditional, or were it in any point doubtful, it would be natural to utter ejaculations, and to seek sympathy. But where the ruin is understood to be absolute, where sympathy cannot be consolation, and counsel cannot be hope, this is otherwise. The voice perishes; the gestures are frozen; and the spirit of man flies back upon its own centre. I, at least, upon seeing those awful gates closed and hung with draperies of woe, as for a death already past, spoke not, nor started, nor groaned. One profound sigh ascended from my heart, and I was silent for days.

It is the record of this third or final stage of opium, as one differing in something more than degree from the others, that I am now undertaking. But a scruple arises as to the true interpretation of these final symptoms. I have elsewhere explained, that it was no particular purpose of mine, and *why* it was no particular purpose, to warn other opium-eaters. Still, as some few persons may use the record in that way, it becomes a matter of interest to ascertain how far it is likely, that, even with the same excesses, other opium-eaters could fall into the same condition. I do not mean to lay a stress upon any supposed idiosyncrasy in myself. Possibly every man has an idiosyncrasy. In some things, undoubtedly, he has. For no man ever yet resembled another man so far, as not to differ from him in features innumerable of his inner nature. But what I point to are hot peculiarities of temperament or of organization, so much as peculiar circumstances and incidents through which my own separate experience had revolved. Some of these were of a nature to alter the whole economy of my mind. Great convulsions, from whatever cause, —from conscience, from fear, from grief, from struggles of the will,- sometimes, in passing away themselves, do not carry off the changes which they have worked. *All* the agitations of this magnitude which a man may have threaded in his life, he neither ought to report, nor *could* report. But one which affected my childhood is a privileged exception. It is privileged as a proper communication for a stranger's ear; because, though relating to a man's proper self, it is a self so far removed from his present self as to wound no feelings of delicacy or just reserve. It is privileged, also, as a proper subject for the sympathy of the narrator. An adult sympathizes with himself in childhood because he is the same, and because (being the same) yet he is *not* the same. He acknowledges the deep, mysterious identity between himself, as adult and as infant, for the ground of his sympathy; and yet, with this general agreement, and necessity of agreement, he feels the differences between his two selves as the main quickeners of his sympathy. He pities the infirmities, as they arise to light in his young forerunner, which now, perhaps, he does not share; he looks indulgently upon the errors of the understanding, or limitations of view which now he has long survived; and sometimes, also, he honors in the infant that rectitude of will which, under *some* temptations, he may since have felt it so difficult to maintain.

The particular case to which I refer in my own childhood was one of intolerable grief; a trial, in fact, more severe than many people at *any* age are called upon to stand. The relation in which the case stands to my latter opium experiences is this: -Those vast clouds of. gloomy grandeur which overhung my dreams at all stages of opium, but which grew into the darkest of miseries in the last, and that haunting of the human face, which latterly towered into a curse, - were they not partly derived from this childish experience? It is certain that, from the essential solitude in which my childhood was passed; from the depth of my sensibility; from the exaltation of this by the resistance of an intellect too prematurely developed; it resulted that the terrific grief which I passed through drove a shaft for me into the worlds of death and darkness which never again closed, and through which it might be said that I ascended and descended at will, according to the temper of my spirits. Some of the phenomena developed in my dream-scenery, undoubtedly, do but repeat the experiences of childhood; and others seem likely to have been growths and fructifications from seeds at that time sown.

The reasons, therefore, for prefixing some account of a "passage" in childhood to this record of a dreadful visitation from opium excess are, 1st, That, in coloring, it harmonizes with that record, and, therefore, is related to it at least in point of feeling; 2dly, That, possibly, it was in part the origin of some features in that record, and so far is related to it in logic; 3dly, That, the final assault of opium being of a nature to challenge the attention of medical men, it is important to clear away all doubts and scruples which can gather about the roots of such a malady. Was it opium, or was it opium in combination with something else, that raised these storms?

Some cynical reader will object, that for this last purpose for would have been sufficient to state the fact, without rehearsing in *extenso* the particulars of that case in childhood. But the reader of more kindness (for a surly reader is always a bad critic) will also have more discernment; and he will perceive that it is not for the mere facts that the case is reported, but because these facts move through a wilderness of natural thoughts or feelings: some in the child who suffers; some in the man who reports; but all so far interesting as they relate to solemn objects. Meantime, the objection of the sullen critic reminds me of a scene sometimes beheld at the English lakes. Figure to yourself an energetic tourist, who protests everywhere that he comes only to see the lakes. He has no business whatever; he is not searching for any recreant indorser of a bill, but simply in search of the picturesque. Yet this man adjures every landlord, "by the virtue of his oath," to tell him, and, as he hopes for peace in this world, to tell him truly, which is the *nearest* road to Keswick. Next, he applies to the postilions,—the Westmoreland postilions always fly down hills at full stretch without locking,—but, nevertheless, in the full career of their fiery race, our picturesque man lets down the glasses, pulls up four horses and two postilions, at the risk of six necks and twenty legs, adjuring them to reveal whether they are taking the shortest road. Finally, he descries my unworthy self upon the road; and, instantly stopping his flying equipage, he demands of me (as one whom he believes to be a scholar and a man of honor) whether there is not, in the possibility of things, a *shorter* cut to Keswick. Now, the answer which rises to the lips of landlord, two postilions, and myself, is this: "Most excellent stranger, as you come to the lakes simply to see their loveliness, might it not be as well to ask after the most beautiful road, rather than the shortest? Because, if abstract shortness, if brevity is your object, then the shortest of all possible tours would seem, with submission, never to have left London." On the same principle, I tell my critic that the whole course of this narrative resembles, and was meant to resemble, a caduceus wreathed about with meandering ornaments, or the shaft of a tree's stem hung round and surmounted with some vagrant parasitical plant. The mere medical subject of the opium answers to the dry, withered pole, which shoots all the rings of the flowering plants, and seems to do so by some dexterity of its own; whereas, in fact, the plant and its tendrils have curled round the sullen cylinder by mere luxuriance of *theirs*. Just as in Cheapside, if you look right and left, the streets so narrow, that lead off at right angles, seem quarried and blasted out of some Babylonian brick-kiln; bored, not raised artificially by the builder's hand. But, if you inquire of the worthy men who live in that neighborhood, you will find it unanimously deposed —that not the streets were quarried out of the bricks, but, on the contrary (most ridiculous as it seems), that the bricks have supervened upon the streets.

The streets did not intrude amongst the bricks, but those cursed bricks came to imprison the streets. So, also, the ugly pole- hop-pole, vine-pole, espalier, no matter what—is there only for support. Not the flowers are for the, pole, but the pole is for the flowers. Upon the same analogy, view me as one (in the words of a true and most impassioned poet [2]) "*viridantem floribus hastas*" — making verdant, and gay with the life of flowers, murderous spears and halberts—things that express death in their origin (being made from dead substances that once had lived in forests), things that express ruin in their use. The true object in my "Opium Confessions" is not the naked physiological theme,—on the contrary, *that* is the ugly pole, the murderous spear, the halbert,— but those wandering musical variations upon the theme,—those parasitical thoughts, feelings, digressions, which climb up with bells and blossoms round about the arid stock; ramble away from it at times with perhaps too rank a luxuriance; but at the same time, by the eternal interest attached to the *subjects* of these digressions, no matter what were the execution, spread a glory over incidents that for themselves would be less than nothing.

[2] Valerius Flaccus.

SUSPIRIA DE PROFUNDIS

PART I

THE AFFLICTION OF CHILDHOOD

IT is so painful to a lover of open-hearted sincerity that any indirect traits of vanity should even *seem* to creep into records of profound passion; and yet, on the other hand, it is so impossible, without an unnatural restraint upon the freedom of the narrative, to prevent oblique gleams reaching the reader from such circumstances of luxury or elegance as did really surround my childhood, that on all accounts I think it better to tell him, from the first, with the simplicity of truth, in what order of society my family moved at the time from which this preliminary narrative is dated. Otherwise it would happen that, merely by moving truly and faithfully through the circumstances of this early experience, I could hardly prevent the reader from receiving an impression as of some higher rank than did really belong to my family. My father was a merchant; not in the sense of Scotland, where it means a man who sells groceries in a cellar, but in the English sense, a sense severely exclusive—namely, he was a man engaged in *foreign* commerce, and no other; therefore, in *wholesale* commerce, and no other,—which last circumstance it is important to mention, because it brings him within the benefit of Cicero's condescending distinction [3]—as one to be despised, certainly, but not too intensely to be despised even by a Roman senator. He—this imperfectly despicable man—died at an early age, and very soon after the incidents here recorded, leaving to his family, then consisting of a wife and six children, an unburthened estate producing exactly £1600 a year. Naturally, therefore, at the date of my narrative,—if narrative it can be called,—he had an income still larger, from the addition of current commercial profits. Now, to any man who is acquainted with commercial life, but, above all, with such life in England, it will readily occur that in an opulent English family of that class,—opulent, though not rich in a mercantile estimate,—the domestic economy is likely to be upon a scale of liberality altogether unknown amongst the corresponding orders in foreign nations. Whether as to the establishment of servants, or as to the provision made for the comfort of all its members, such a household not uncommonly eclipses the scale of living even amongst the poorer classes of our nobility, though the most splendid in Europe—a fact which, since the period of my infancy, I have had many personal opportunities for verifying both in England and in Ireland. From this peculiar anomaly, affecting the domestic economy of merchants, there arises a disturbance upon the general scale of outward signs by which we measure the relations of rank. The equation, so to speak, between one order He gives a real merchant (one who is such in the English sense) leave to think himself a shade above small beer. of society and another, which usually travels in the natural line of their comparative expenditure, is here interrupted and defeated, so that one rank would be collected from the name of the occupation, and another rank, much higher, from the splendor of the domestic *ménage*. I warn the reader, therefore (or, rather, my explanation has already warned him), that he is not to infer, from any casual gleam of luxury or elegance, a corresponding elevation of rank.

[3] Cicero, in a well-known passage of his *Ethics*, speaks of trade as irredeemably base, if petty; but as not so absolutely felonius if wholesale. He gives a *real* merchant (one who is

such in the English sense) leave to think himself a shade above small-beer.

We, the children of the house, stood in fact upon the very happiest tier in the scaffolding of society for all good influences. The prayer of Agar—"Give me neither poverty nor riches"— was realized for us. That blessing had we, being neither too high nor too low: high enough we were to see models of good manners; obscure enough to be left in the sweetest of solitudes. Amply furnished with the nobler benefits of wealth, *extra* means of health, of intellectual culture, and of elegant enjoyment, on the other hand, we knew nothing of its social distinctions. Not depressed by the consciousness of privations too sordid, not tempted into restlessness by the consciousness of privileges too aspiring, we had no motives for shame, we had none for pride. Grateful also to this hour I am; that, amidst luxuries in all things else, we were trained to a Spartan simplicity of diet,—that we fared, in fact, very much less sumptuously than the servants. And if (after the model of the Emperor Marcus Aurelius) I should return thanks to Providence for all the separate blessings of my early situation, these four I would single out as chiefly worthy to be commemorated—that I lived in the country; that I lived in solitude; that my infant feelings were moulded by the gentlest of sisters, not by horrid pugilistic brothers; finally, that I and they were dutiful children, of a pure, holy, and magnificent church.

The earliest incidents in my life which affected me so deeply as to be rememberable at this day were two, and both before I could have completed my second year; namely, a remarkable dream of terrific grandeur about a favorite nurse, which is interesting for a reason to be noticed hereafter; and, secondly, the fact of having connected a profound sense of pathos with the reappearance, very early in the spring, of some crocuses. This I mention as inexplicable, for such annual resurrections of plants and flowers affect us only as memorials, or suggestions of a higher change, and therefore in connection with the idea of death; but of death I could, at that time, have had no experience whatever.

This, however, I was speedily to acquire. My two eldest sisters—eldest of three *then* living, and also elder than myself—were summoned to an early death. The first who died was Jane, about a year older than myself. She was three and a half, I two and a half, *plus* or *minus* some trifle that I do not recollect. But death was then scarcely intelligible to me, and I could not so properly be said to suffer sorrow as a sad perplexity. There was another death in the house about the same time, namely, of a maternal grandmother; but as she had in a manner come to us for the express purpose of dying in her daughter's society, and from illness had lived perfectly secluded, our nursery party knew her but little, and were certainly more affected by the death (which I witnessed) of a favorite bird, namely, a kingfisher who had been injured by an accident. With my sister Jane's death (though otherwise, as I have said, less sorrowful than unintelligible) there was, however, connected an incident which made a most fearful impression upon myself, deepening my tendencies to thoughtfulness and abstraction beyond what would seem credible for my years. If there was one thing in this world from which, more than from any other, nature had forced me to revolt, it was brutality and violence. Now, a whisper arose in the family that a woman-servant, who by accident was drawn off from her proper duties to attend my sister Jane for a day or two, had on one occasion treated her harshly, if not brutally; and as this ill treatment happened within two days of her death, so that the occasion of it must have been some fretfulness in the poor child caused by her sufferings, naturally there was a sense of awe diffused through the family. I believe the story never reached my mother, and possibly it was exaggerated; but upon me the effect was terrific.

I did not often see the person charged with this cruelty; but, when I did, my eyes sought the ground; nor could I have borne to look her in the face—not through anger; and as to vindictive thoughts, how could these lodge in a powerless infant? The feeling which fell upon me was a shuddering awe, as upon a first glimpse of the truth that I was in a world of evil and strife. Though born in a large town, I had passed the whole of my childhood, except for the few earliest weeks, in a rural seclusion. With three innocent little sisters for playmates, sleeping always amongst them, and shut up forever in a silent garden from all knowledge of poverty, or oppression, or outrage, I had not suspected until this moment the true complexion of the world in which myself and my sisters were living. Henceforward the character of my thoughts must have changed greatly; for so *representative* are some acts, that one single case of the class is sufficient to throw open before you the whole theatre of possibilities in that direction. I never heard that the woman, accused of this cruelty, took it at all to heart, even after the event which so immediately succeeded had reflected upon it a more painful emphasis. On the other hand, I knew of a case, and will pause to mention it, where a mere semblance and shadow of such cruelty, under similar circumstances, inflicted the grief of self-reproach through the remainder of life. A boy, interesting in his appearance, as also from his remarkable docility, was attacked, on a cold day of spring, by a complaint of the trachea—not precisely croup, but like it. He was three years old, and had been ill perhaps for four days; but at intervals had been in high spirits, and capable of playing. This sunshine, gleaming through dark clouds, had continued even on the fourth day; and from nine to eleven o'clock at night he had showed more animated pleasure than ever. An old servant, hearing of his illness, had called to see him; and her mode of talking with him had excited all the joyousness of his nature. About midnight, his mother, fancying that his feet felt cold, was muffling them up in flannels; and, as he seemed to resist her a little, she struck lightly on the sole of one foot as a mode of admonishing him to be quiet. He did not repeat his motion; and in less than a minute his mother had him in her arms with his face looking upwards. "What is the meaning," she exclaimed, in sudden affright, "of this strange repose settling upon his features?" She called loudly to a servant in another room; but before the servant could reach her, the child had drawn two inspirations, deep, yet gentle—and had died in his mother's arms! Upon this, the poor afflicted lady made the discovery that those struggles, which she had supposed to be expressions of resistance to herself, were the struggles of departing life. It followed, or seemed to follow, that with these final struggles had blended an expression, on *her* part, of displeasure. Doubtless the child had not distinctly perceived it; but the mother could never look back to that incident without self-reproach. And seven years after, when her own death happened, no progress had been made in reconciling her thoughts to that which only the depth of love could have viewed as an offence.

So passed away from earth one out of those sisters that made up my nursery playmates; and so did my acquaintance (if such it could be called) commence with mortality. Yet, in fact, I knew little more of mortality than that Jane had disappeared. She had gone away; but, perhaps, she would come back. Happy interval of heaven-born ignorance! Gracious immunity of infancy from sorrow disproportioned to its strength! I was sad for Jane's absence. But still in my heart I trusted that she would come again. Summer and winter came again— crocuses and roses; why not little Jane?

Thus easily was healed, then, the first wound in my infant heart. Not so the second. For thou, dear, noble Elizabeth, around whose ample brow, as often as thy sweet countenance rises upon the darkness, I fancy a tiara of light or a gleaming *aureola* in token of thy premature intellectual grandeur,—thou whose head, for its superb developments, was the astonishment of science [4],—thou next, but after an interval of happy years, thou also wert summoned away from our nursery; and the night which, for me, gathered upon that event, ran after my steps far into life; and perhaps at this day I resemble little for good or for ill that which else I should have been. Pillar of fire that didst go before me to guide and to quicken,— pillar of darkness, when thy countenance was turned away to God, that didst too truly shed the shadow of death over my young heart,—in what scales should I weigh thee? Was the blessing greater from thy heavenly presence, or the blight which followed thy departure? Can a man weigh off and value the glories of dawn against the darkness of hurricane? Or, if he could, how is it that, when a memorable love has been followed by a memorable bereavement, even suppose that God would replace the sufferer in a point of time anterior to the entire experience, and offer to cancel the woe, but so that the sweet face which had caused the woe should also be obliterated, vehemently would every man shrink from the exchange! In the Paradise Lost, this strong instinct of man, to prefer the heavenly, mixed and polluted with the earthly, to a level experience offering neither one nor the other, is divinely commemorated. What words of pathos are in that speech of Adam's—If God should make another Eve," &c.; that is, if God should replace him in his primitive state, and should condescend to bring again a second Eve, one that would listen to no temptation, still that original partner of his earliest solitude—

> "Creature in whom excelled
> Whatever can to sight or thought be formed,
> Holy, divine, good, amiable, or sweet"—

even now, when she appeared in league with an eternity of woe, and ministering to his ruin, could not be displaced for him by any better or happier Eve. "Loss of thee!" he exclaims, in this anguish of trial—

> "Loss of thee
> Would never from my heart; no, no, I feel
> The link of nature draw me; flesh of flesh,
> Bone of my bone thou art; and from thy state
> Mine never shall be parted, bliss or woe [5]."

[4] *"The astonishment of science."*—Her medical attendants were Dr Percival, a well-known literary physician, who had been a correspondent of Condorcet, D'Alembert, &c., and Mr Charles White, a very distinguished surgeon. It was he who pronounced her head to be the finest in its structure and development of any that he had ever seen—an assertion which, to my knowledge, he repeated in after years, and with enthusiasm. That he had some acquaintance with the subject may be presumed from this, that he wrote and published a work on he human skull, supported by many measurements which he had made of heads selected from all varieties of the human species. Meantime, as I would be loth that any trait of what might seem vanity should creep into this record, I will candidly admit that she died of hydrocephalus; and it has often been supposed that the premature expansion of the intellect in cases of that class, is altogether morbid—forced on, in fact, by the mere stimulation of the disease. I would, however, suggest, as a possibility, the very inverse order of relation

between the disease and the intellectual manifestations. Not the disease may always have caused the preternatural growth of the intellect, but, on the contrary, this growth coming on spontaneously, and outrunning the capacities of the physical structure, may have caused the disease.

[5] Amongst the oversights in the *Paradise Lost*, some of which have not yet been perceived, it is certainly *one*—that, by placing in such overpowering light of pathos the sublime sacrifice of Adam to his love for his frail companion, he has too much lowered the guilt of his disobedience to God. All that Milton can say afterwards, does not, and cannot, obscure the beauty of that action: reviewing it calmly, we condemn—but taking the impassioned station of Adam at the moment of temptation, we approve in our hearts. This was certainly an oversight; but it was one very difficult to redress. I remember, amongst the many exquisite thoughts of John Paul, (Richter,) one which strikes me as particularly touching upon this subject. He suggests—not as any grave theological comment, but as the wandering fancy of a poetic heart—that, had Adam conquered the anguish of separation as a pure sacrifice of obedience to God, his reward would have been the pardon and reconciliation of Eve, together with her restoration to innocence.

But what was it that drew my heart, by gravitation so strong, to my sister? Could a child, little above six years of age, place any special value upon her intellectual forwardness? Serene and capacious as her mind appeared to me upon after review, was *that* a charm for stealing away the heart of an infant? O, no! I think of it *now* with interest, because it lends, in a stranger's ear, some justification to the excess of my fondness. But then it was lost upon me; or, if not lost, was but dimly perceived. Hadst thou been an idiot, my sister, not the less I must have loved thee, having that capacious heart overflowing, even as mine overflowed, with tenderness, and stung, even as mine was stung, by the necessity of being loved. This it was which crowned thee with beauty—

> "Love, the holy sense,
> Best gift of God, in thee was most intense."

That lamp lighted in Paradise was kindled for me which shone so steadily in thee; and never but to thee only, never again since thy departure, *durst* I utter the feelings which possessed me. For I was the shyest of children; and a natural sense of personal dignity held me back at all stages of life, from exposing the least ray of feelings which I was not encouraged *wholly* to reveal.

It would be painful, and it is needless, to pursue the course of that sickness which carried off my leader and companion. She (according to my recollection at this moment) was just as much above eight years as I above six. And perhaps this natural precedency of authority in judgment, and the tender humility with which she declined to assert it, had been amongst the fascinations of her presence. It was upon a Sunday evening, or so people fancied, that the spark of fatal fire fell upon that train of predispositions to a brain complaint which had hitherto slumbered within her. She had been permitted to drink tea at the house of a laboring man, the father of an old female servant. The sun had set when she returned in the company of this servant through meadows reeking with exhalations after a fervent day. From that time she sickened. Happily, a child in such circumstances feels no anxieties. Looking upon medical men as people whose natural commission it is to heal diseases, since it is their natural function to profess it, knowing them only as *ex officio* privileged to make war upon pain and sickness, I never had a misgiving about the result. I grieved, indeed, that my sister should lie in bed; I grieved still more sometimes to hear her moan. But all this appeared to me no more than a night of trouble, on which the dawn would soon arise. O! moment of darkness and delirium, when a nurse awakened me from that delusion, and launched God's thunderbolt at my heart in the assurance that my sister must die. Rightly it is said of utter, utter misery, that it " cannot be *remembered*. [6] "Itself, as a remarkable thing, is swallowed up in its own chaos. Mere anarchy and confusion of mind fell upon me. Deaf and blind I was, as I reeled under the revelation. I wish not to recall the circumstances of that time, when my agony was at its height, and hers in another sense was approaching. Enough to say, that all was soon over; and the morning of that day had at last arrived which looked down upon her innocent face, sleeping the sleep from which there is no awaking, and upon me sorrowing the sorrow for which there is no consolation.

[6] "I stood in unimaginable trance
    And agony, which cannot be remember'd."
    —*Speech of Alhadra in Coleridge's Remorse.*

On the day after my sister's death, whilst the sweet temple of her brain was yet unviolated by human scrutiny, I formed my own scheme for seeing her once more. Not for the world would I have made this known, nor have suffered a witness to accompany me. I had never heard of feelings that take the name of "sentimental," nor dreamed of such a possibility. But grief even in a child hates the light, and shrinks from human eyes. The house was large; there were two staircases; and by one of these I knew that about noon, when all would be quiet, I could steal up into her chamber. I imagine that it was exactly high noon when I reached the chamber door; it was locked, but the key was not taken away. Entering, I closed the door so softly, that, although it opened upon a hall which ascended through all the stories, no echo ran along the silent walls. Then turning round, I sought my sister's face. But the bed had been moved, and the back was now turned. Nothing met my eyes but one large window wide open, through which the sun of midsummer at noonday was showering down torrents of splendor. The weather was dry, the sky was cloudless, the blue depths seemed the express types of infinity; and it was not possible for eye to behold or for heart to conceive any symbols more pathetic of life and the glory of life.

Let me pause for one instant in approaching a remembrance so affecting and revolutionary for my own mind, and one which (if any earthly remembrance) will survive for me in the hour of death,—to remind some readers, and to inform others, that in the original *Opium Confessions* I endeavored to explain the reason [7] why death, *caeteris paribus*, is more profoundly affecting in summer than in other parts of the year; so far, at least, as it is liable to any modification at all from accidents of scenery or season. The reason, as I there suggested, lies in the antagonism between the tropical redundancy of life in summer and the dark sterilities of the grave. The summer we see, the grave we haunt with our thoughts; the glory is around us, the darkness is within us. And the two coming into collision, each exalts the other into stronger relief. But in my case there was even a subtler reason why the summer had this intense power of vivifying the spectacle or the thoughts of death. And, recollecting it, often I have been struck with the important truth, that far more of our deepest thoughts and feelings pass to us through perplexed combinations of *concrete* objects, pass to us as *involutes* (if I may coin that word) in compound experiences incapable of being disentangled, than ever reach us *directly*, and in their own abstract shapes. It had happened that amongst our nursery collection of books was the Bible illustrated with many pictures. And in long dark evenings, as my three sisters with myself sate by the firelight round the *guard* of our nursery, no book was so much in request amongst us. It ruled us and swayed us as mysteriously as music. One young nurse, whom we all loved, before any candle was lighted, would often strain her eye to read it for us; and, sometimes, according to her simple powers, would endeavor to explain what we found obscure. We, the children, were all constitutionally touched with pensiveness; the fitful gloom and sudden lambencies of the room by firelight suited our evening state of feelings; and they suited, also, the divine revelations of power and mysterious beauty which awed us. Above all, the story of a just man—man and yet not man, real above all things, and yet shadowy above all things, who had suffered the passion of death in Palestine—slept upon our minds like early dawn upon the waters. The nurse knew and explained to us the chief differences in oriental climates; and all these differences (as it happens) express themselves in the great varieties of summer. The cloudless sunlights of Syria—those seemed to argue everlasting summer; the disciples plucking the ears of corn—that must be summer; but, above all, the very name of Palm Sunday (a festival in the English church) troubled me like an anthem. "Sunday!" what was *that*? That was the day of peace which masked another peace deeper than the heart of man can comprehend. "Palms!" what were they? That was an equivocal word; palms, in the sense of trophies, expressed the pomps of life; palms, as a product of nature, expressed the pomps of summer. Yet still even this explanation does not suffice; it was not merely by the peace and by the summer, by the deep sound of rest below all rest, and of ascending glory, that I had been haunted. It was also because Jerusalem stood near to those deep images both in time and in place. The great event of Jerusalem was at hand when Palm Sunday came; and the scene of that Sunday was near in place to Jerusalem; Yet what then was Jerusalem? Did I fancy it to be the *omphalos* (navel) of the earth? That pretension had once been made for Jerusalem, and once for Delphi; and both pretensions had become ridiculous, as the figure of the planet became known. Yes; but if not of the earth, for earth's tenant, Jerusalem was the *omphalos* of mortality. Yet how? there, on the contrary, it was, as we infants understood, that mortality had been trampled under foot. True; but, for that very reason, there it was that mortality had opened its very gloomiest crater. There it was, indeed, that the human had risen on wings from the grave; but, for that reason, there also it was that the divine had been swallowed up by the abyss; the lesser star could not rise, before the greater would submit to eclipse. Summer, therefore, had connected itself with death, not merely as a mode of antagonism, but also through intricate relations to scriptural scenery and events.

[7] Some readers will question the *fact*, and seek no reason. But did they ever suffer grief at *any* season of the year?

Out of this digression, which was almost necessary for the purpose of showing how inextricably my feelings and images of death were entangled with those of summer, I return to the bed-chamber of my sister. From the gorgeous sunlight I turned round to the corpse. There lay the sweet childish figure; there the angel face; and, as people usually fancy, it was said in the house that no features had suffered any change. Had they not? The forehead, indeed,—the serene and noble forehead,—*that* might be the same; but the frozen eyelids, the darkness that seemed to steal from beneath them, the marble lips, the stiffening hands, laid palm to palm, as if repeating the supplications of closing anguish,—could these be mistaken for life? Had it been so, wherefore did I not spring to those heavenly lips with tears and never-ending kisses? But so it was *not*. I stood checked for a moment; awe, not fear, fell upon me; and, whilst I stood, a solemn wind began to blow,—the most mournful that ear ever heard. Mournful! that is saying nothing. It was a wind that had swept the fields of mortality for a hundred centuries. Many times since, upon a summer day, when the sun is about the hottest, I have remarked the same wind arising and uttering the same hollow, solemn, Memnonian, but saintly swell: it is in this world the one sole *audible* symbol of eternity. And three times in my life I have happened to hear the same sound in the same circumstances, namely, when standing between an open window and a dead body on a summer day.

Instantly, when my ear caught this vast Æolian intonation, when my eye filled with the golden fullness of life, the pomps and glory of the heavens outside, and turning when it settled upon the frost which overspread my sister's face, instantly a trance fell upon me. A vault seemed to open in the zenith of the far blue sky, a shaft which ran up forever. I, in spirit, rose as if on billows that also ran up the shaft forever; and the billows seemed to pursue the throne of God; but *that* also ran before us and fled away continually. The flight and the pursuit seemed to go on for ever and ever. Frost, gathering frost, some Sarsar wind of death, seemed to repel me; I slept - for how long I cannot say: slowly I recovered my self-possession, and found myself standing, as before, close to my sister's bed.

Oh [8] flight of the solitary child to the solitary God—flight from the ruined corpse to the throne that could not be ruined!—how rich wert thou in truth for after years! Rupture of grief that, being too mighty for a child to sustain, foundest a happy oblivion in a heaven-born dream, and within that sleep didst conceal a dream, whose meaning, in after years, when slowly I deciphered, suddenly there flashed upon me new light; and even by the grief of a child, as I will show you, reader, hereafter, were confounded the falsehoods of philosophers [9].

[8] Φυγη μονου προς μονον.—PLOTINUS.
[9] The thoughts referred to will be given in final notes; as at this point they seemed too much to interrupt the course of the narrative.

In the *Opium Confessions* I touched a little upon the extraordinary power connected with opium (after long use) of amplifying the dimensions of time. Space, also, it amplifies by degrees that are sometimes terrific. But time it is upon which the exalting and multiplying power of opium chiefly spends its operation. Time becomes infinitely elastic, stretching out to such immeasurable and vanishing termini, that it seems ridiculous to compute the sense of it, on waking, by expressions commensurate to human life. As in starry fields one computes by diameters of the earth's orbit, or of Jupiter's, so, in valuing the virtual time lived during some dreams, the measurement by generations is ridiculous—by millenia is ridiculous; by eons, I should say, if eons were more determinate, would be also, ridiculous. On this single occasion, however, in my life, the very inverse phenomenon occurred. But why speak of it in connection with opium? Could a child of six years old have been under that influence? No, but simply because it so exactly reversed the operation of opium. Instead of a short interval expanding into a vast one, upon this occasion a long one had contracted into a minute. I have reason to believe that a *very* long one had elapsed during this wandering or suspension of my perfect mind. When I returned to myself, there was a foot (or I fancied so) on the stairs. I was alarmed; for I believed that, if anybody should detect me, means would be taken to prevent my coming again. Hastily, therefore, I kissed the lips that I should kiss no more, and slunk like a guilty thing with stealthy steps from the room. Thus perished the vision, loveliest amongst all the shows which earth has revealed to me; thus mutilated was the parting which should have lasted forever; thus tainted with fear was the farewell sacred to love and grief, to perfect love and perfect grief.

O, Ahasuerus, everlasting Jew [10]! fable or not a fable, thou when first starting on thy endless pilgrimage of woe,—thou when first flying through the gates of Jerusalem, and vainly yearning to leave the pursuing curse behind thee, couldst not more certainly have read thy doom of sorrow in the misgivings of thy troubled brain than I when passing forever from my sister's room. The worm was at my heart; and, confining myself to that state of life, I may say—the worm that could not die. For if, when standing upon the threshold of manhood, I had ceased to feel its perpetual gnawings, *that* was because a vast expansion of intellect, it was because new hopes, new necessities, and the frenzy of youthful blood, had translated me into a new creature. Man is doubtless one by some subtle *nexus* that we cannot perceive, extending from the newborn infant to the superannuated dotard: but as regards many affections and passions incident to his nature at different stages, he is *not* one; the unity of man in this respect is coextensive only with the particular stage to which the passion belongs. Some passions, as that of sexual love, are celestial by one half of their origin, animal and earthly by the other half. These will not survive their own appropriate stage. But love, which is *altogether* holy, like that between two children, will. revisit undoubtedly by glimpses the silence and the darkness of old age: and I repeat my belief—that, unless bodily torment should forbid it, that final experience in my sister's bed-room, or some other in which her innocence was concerned, will rise again for me, to illuminate the hour of death.

[10] "Everlasting Jew!"—*der ewige Jude*—which is the common German expression for
   The Wandering Jew, and sublime even than our own.

On the day following this which I have recorded, came a body of medical men to examine the brain, and the particular nature of the complaint, for in some of its symptoms it had shown perplexing anomalies. Such is the sanctity of death, and especially of death alighting on an innocent child, that even gossiping people do not gossip on such a subject. Consequently, I knew nothing of the purpose which drew together these surgeons, nor suspected anything of the cruel changes which might have been wrought in my sister's head. Long after this, I saw a similar case; I surveyed the corpse (it was that of a beautiful boy, eighteen years old, who had died of the same complaint) one hour *after* the surgeons had laid the skull in ruins; but the dishonors of this scrutiny were hidden by bandages, and had not disturbed the repose of the countenance. So it might have been here; but, if it were *not* so, then I was happy in being spared the shock, from having that marble image of peace, icy and rigid as it was, unsettled by disfiguring images. Some hours after the strangers had withdrawn, I crept again to the room; but the door was now locked—the key was taken away—and I was shut out forever.

Then came the funeral. I, as a point of decorum, was carried thither. I was put into a carriage with some gentlemen whom I did not know. They were kind to me; but naturally they talked of things disconnected with the occasion, and their conversation was a torment. At the church, I was told to hold a white handkerchief to my eyes. Empty hypocrisy! What need had *he* of masques or mockeries, whose heart died within him at every word that was uttered? During that part of the service which passed within the church, I made an effort to attend; but I sank back continually into my own solitary darkness, and I heard little consciously, except some fugitive strains from the sublime chapter of St. Paul, which in England is always read at burials. And here I notice a profound error of our present illustrious laureate. When I heard those dreadful words,— for dreadful they were to me, "It is sown in corruption, it is raised in incorruption; it is sown in dishonor, it is raised in glory;" such was the recoil of my feelings, that I could even have shrieked out a protesting—"O, no, no!" if I had not been restrained by the publicity of the occasion. In after years, reflecting upon this revolt of my feelings, which, being the voice of nature in a child, must be as true as any mere *opinion* of a child might probably be false, I saw, at once, the unsoundness of a passage in *The Excursion*. The book is not here, but the substance I remember perfectly. Mr. Wordsworth argues, that if it were not for the unsteady faith which people fix upon the beatific condition after death of those whom they deplore, nobody could be found so selfish as even secretly to wish for the restoration to earth of a beloved object. A mother, for instance, could never dream of yearning for her child, and secretly calling it back by her silent aspirations from the arms of God, if she were but reconciled to the belief that really it was in those arms. But this I utterly deny. To take my own case, when I heard those dreadful words of St. Paul applied to my sister, namely, that she should be raised a spiritual body, nobody can suppose that selfishness, or any other feeling than that of agonizing love, caused the rebellion of my heart against them. I knew already that she was to come again in beauty and power. I did not now learn this for the first time. And that thought, doubtless, made my sorrow sublimer; but also it made it deeper. For here lay the sting of it, namely, in the fatal words—"We shall be *changed*." How was the unity of my interest in her to be preserved, if she were to be altered, and no longer to reflect in her sweet countenance the traces that were sculptured on my heart? Let a magician ask any woman whether she will permit him to improve her child, to raise it even from deformity to perfect beauty, if that must be done at the cost of its identity, and there is no loving mother but would reject his proposal with horror. Or, to take a case that has actually happened, if a mother were robbed of her child, at two years old, by gypsies, and the same child were restored to her at twenty, a fine young man, but divided by a sleep as it were of death from all remembrances that could restore the broken links of their once tender connection, would she not feel her grief unhealed, and her heart defrauded? Undoubtedly she would. All of us ask not of God for a better thing than that we have lost; we ask for the same, even with its faults and its frailties. It is true, that the sorrowing person will also be changed eventually, but that must be by death. And a prospect so remote as that, and so alien from our present nature, cannot console us in an affliction which is not remote, but present— which is not spiritual, but human.

Lastly came the magnificent service which the English Church performs at the side of the grave. There is exposed once again, and for the last time, the coffin. All eyes survey the record of name, of sex, of age, and the day of departure from earth,—records how useless! and dropped into darkness as if messages addressed to worms. Almost at the very last comes the symbolic ritual, tearing and shattering the heart with volleying discharges, peal after peal, from the final artillery of woe. The coffin is lowered into its home; it has disappeared from the eye. The sacristan stands ready, with his shovel of earth and stones. The priest's voice is heard once more,—*earth* to *earth*, and the dread rattle ascends from the lid of the coffin; *ashes* to *ashes*, and again the killing sound is heard; *dust* to *dust*, and the farewell volley announces that the grave—the coffin - the face are sealed up for ever and ever.

Oh, grief! thou art classed amongst the depressing passions. And true it is, that thou humblest to the dust, but also thou exaltest to the clouds. Thou shakest as with ague, but also thou steadiest like frost. Thou sickenest the heart, but also thou healest its infirmities. Among the very foremost of mine was morbid sensibility to shame. And, ten years afterwards, I used to reproach myself with this infirmity, by supposing the case, that, if it were thrown upon me to seek aid for a perishing fellow-creature, and that I could obtain that aid only by facing a vast company of critical or sneering faces, I might, perhaps, shrink basely from the duty. It is true, that no such case had ever actually occurred, so that it was a mere romance of casuistry to tax myself with cowardice so shocking. But, to feel a doubt, was to feel condemnation; and the crime which *might* have been was in my eyes the crime which *had* been. Now, however, all was changed; and for anything which regarded my sister's memory, in one hour I received a new heart. Once in Westmoreland I saw a case resembling it. I saw a ewe suddenly put off and abjure her own nature, in a service of love,—yes, slough it as completely as ever serpent sloughed his skin. Her lamb had fallen into a deep trench, from which all escape was hopeless, without the aid of man. And to a man she advanced boldly, bleating clamorously, until he followed her and rescued her beloved. Not less was the change in myself. Fifty thousand sneering faces would not have troubled me in any office of tenderness to my sister's memory. Ten legions would not have repelled me from seeking her, if there was a chance that she could be found. Mockery! it was lost upon me. Laugh at me, as one or two people did! I valued not their laughter. And when I was told insultingly to cease "my girlish tears," that word "*girlish*" had no sting for me, except as a verbal echo to the one eternal thought of my heart,—that a girl was the sweetest thing I, in my short life, had known,—that a girl it was who had crowned the earth with beauty, and had opened to my thirst fountains of pure celestial love, from which, in this world, I was to drink no more.

Interesting it is to observe how certainly all deep feelings agree in this, that they seek for solitude, and are nursed by solitude. Deep grief, deep love, how naturally do these ally themselves with religious feeling; and all three—love, grief, religion—are haunters of solitary places. Love, grief, the passion of reverie, or the mystery of devotion,—what were these, without solitude? All day long, when it was not impossible for me to do so, I sought the most silent and sequestered nooks in the grounds about the house, or in the neighboring fields. The awful stillness occasionally of summer noons, when no winds were abroad, the appealing silence of gray or misty afternoons,—these were fascinations as of witchcraft. Into the woods or the desert air I gazed, as if some comfort lay hid in them. I wearied the heavens with my inquest of beseeching looks. I tormented the blue depths with obstinate scrutiny, sweeping them with my eyes, and searching them forever after one angelic face that might, perhaps, have permission to reveal itself for a moment. The faculty of shaping images in the distance out of slight elements, and grouping them after the yearnings of the heart, aided by a slight defect in my eyes, grew upon me at this time. And I recall at the present moment one instance of that sort, which may show how merely shadows, or a gleam of brightness, or nothing at all, could furnish a sufficient basis for this creative faculty. On Sunday mornings I was always taken to church: it was a church on the old and natural model of England, having aisles, galleries, organs, all things ancient and venerable, and the proportions majestic. Here, whilst the congregation knelt through the long litany, as often as we came to that passage, so beautiful amongst many that are so, where God is supplicated on behalf of "all sick persons and young children," and that he would "show his pity upon all prisoners and captives,"- I wept in secret, and raising my streaming eyes to the windows of the galleries, saw, on days when the sun was shining, a spectacle as affecting as ever prophet can have beheld. The sides of the windows were rich with storied glass; through the deep purples and crimsons streamed the golden light; emblazonries of heavenly illumination mingling with the earthly emblazonries of what is grandest in man. There were the apostles that had trampled upon earth, and the glories of earth, out of celestial love to man. There were the martyrs that had borne witness to the truth through flames, through torments, and through armies of fierce insulting faces. There were the saints who, under intolerable pangs, had glorified God by meek submission to his will. And all the time, whilst this tumult of sublime memorials held on as the deep chords from an accompaniment in the bass, I saw through the wide central field of the window, where the glass was uncolored, white fleecy clouds sailing over the azure depths of the sky; were it but a fragment or a hint of such a cloud, immediately under the flash of my sorrow-haunted eye, it grew and shaped itself into visions of beds with white lawny curtains; and in the beds lay sick children, dying children, that were tossing in anguish, and weeping clamorously for death. God, for some mysterious reason, could not suddenly release them from their pain; but he suffered the beds, as it seemed, to rise slowly through the clouds; slowly the beds ascended into the chambers of the air; slowly, also, his arms descended from the heavens, that he and his young children, whom in Judea, once and forever, he had blessed, though they must pass slowly through the dreadful chasm of separation, might yet meet the sooner. These visions were self-sustained. These visions needed not that any sound should speak to me, or music mould my feelings. The hint from the litany, the fragment from the clouds,— those and the storied windows were sufficient. But not the less the blare of the tumultuous organ wrought its own separate creations. And oftentimes in anthems, when the mighty instrument threw its vast columns of sound, fierce yet melodious, over the voices of the choir,—when it rose high in arches, as might seem, surmounting and overriding the strife of the vocal parts, and gathering by strong coercion the total storm into unity, -sometimes I seemed to walk triumphantly upon those clouds which so recently I had looked up to as mementos of prostrate sorrow, and even as ministers of sorrow in its creations; yes, sometimes under the transfigurations of music I felt [11] of grief itself as a fiery chariot for mounting victoriously above the causes of grief.

[11] "*I felt*."—The reader must not forget, in reading this and other passages, that, though a child's feelings are spoken of, it is not the child who speaks. I decipher what the child only felt in cipher. And so far is this distinction or this explanation from pointing to any thing metaphysical or doubtful, that a man must be grossly unobservant who is not aware of what I am here noticing, not as a peculiarity of this child or that, but as a necessity of all children. Whatsoever in a man's mind blossoms and expands to his own consciousness in mature life, must have pre-existed in germ during his infancy. I, for instance, did not, as a child, *consciously* read in my own deep feelings these ides. No, not at all; now was it possible for a child to do so. I the child had the feelings, I the man decipher them. In the child lay the handwriting mysterious to *him*; in me the interpretation and the comment.

I point so often to the feelings, the ideas, or the ceremonies of religion, because there never yet was profound grief nor profound philosophy which did not inosculate at many points with profound religion. But I request the reader to understand, that of all things I was not, and could not have been, a child trained to talk of religion, least of all to talk of it controversially or polemically. Dreadful is the picture, which in books we sometimes find, of children discussing, the doctrines of Christianity, and even teaching their seniors the boundaries and distinctions between doctrine and doctrine. And it has often struck me with amazement, that the two things which God made most beautiful among his works, namely, infancy and pure religion, should, by the folly of man (in yoking them together on erroneous principles), neutralize each other's beauty, or even form a combination positively hateful. The religion becomes nonsense, and the child becomes a hypocrite. The religion is transfigured into cant, and the innocent child into a dissembling liar [12].

[12] I except, however, one case—the case of a child dying of an organic disorder, so therefore as to die slowly, and aware of its own condition. Because such a child is solemnized, and sometimes, in a partial sense, inspired—inspired by the depth of its sufferings, and by the awfulness of its prospect. Such a child having put off the earthly mind in many things, may naturally have put off the childish mind in all things. I therefore, speaking for myself only, acknowledge to have read with emotion a record of a little girl, who, knowing herself for months to be amongst the elect of death, became anxious even to sickness of heart for what she called the *conversation* of her father. Her filial duty and reverence had been swallowed up in filial love.

God, be assured, takes care for the religion of children, wheresoever his Christianity exists. Wheresoever there is a national church established, to which a child sees his friends resorting,—wheresoever he beholds all whom he honors periodically prostrate before those illimitable heavens which fill to overflowing his young adoring heart,-wheresoever he sees the sleep of death falling at intervals upon men and women whom he knows, depth as confounding to the plummet of his mind as those heavens ascend beyond his power to pursue,—*there* take you no thought for the religion of a child, any more than for the lilies how they shall be arrayed, or for the ravens how they shall feed their young.

God speaks to children, also, in dreams, and by the oracles that lurk in darkness. But in solitude, above all things, when made vocal by the truths and services of a national church, God holds "communion undisturbed" with children. Solitude, though silent as light, is, like light, the mightiest of agencies; for solitude is essential to man. All men come into this world alone; all leave it *alone*. Even a little child has a dread, whispering consciousness, that if he should be summoned to travel into God's presence, no gentle nurse will be allowed to lead him by the hand, nor mother to carry him in her arms, nor little sister to share his trepidations. King and priest, warrior and maiden, childish mind in all things. King and priest, warrior and maiden, philosopher and child, all must walk those mighty galleries alone. The solitude, therefore, which in this world appals or fascinates a child's heart, is but the echo of a far deeper solitude through which already he has passed, and of another solitude, deeper still, through which he has to pass: reflex of one solitude—prefiguration of another.

O, burthen of solitude, that cleavest to man through every stage of his being! in his birth, which *has* been,—in his life, which is,—in his death, which *shall* be, mighty and essential solitude! that wast, and art, and art to be;—thou broodest, like the spirit of God moving upon the surface of the deeps, over every heart that sleeps in the nurseries of

Christendom. Like the vast laboratory of the air, which, seeming to be nothing, or less than the shadow of a shade, hides within itself the principles of all things, solitude for. the child is the Agrippa's mirror of the unseen universe. Deep is the solitude in life of millions upon millions, who, with hearts welling forth love, have none to love them. Deep is the solitude of those who, with secret griefs, have none to pity them. Deep is the solitude of those who, fighting with doubts or darkness, have none to counsel them. But deeper than the deepest of these solitudes is that which broods over childhood, bringing before it, at intervals, the final solitude which watches for it, and is waiting for it within the gates of death. Reader, I tell you a truth, and hereafter I will convince you of this truth, that for a Grecian child solitude was nothing, but for a Christian child it has become the power of God and the mystery of God. O, mighty and essential solitude, that wast, and art, and art to be! thou, kindling under the torch of Christian revelations, art now transfigured forever, and hast passed from a blank negation into a secret hieroglyphic from God, shadowing in the hearts of infancy the very dimmest of his truths!

"*But you forget her,*" says the cynic; "*you happened one day to forget this sister of yours?*" Why not? To cite the beautiful words of Wallenstein,

> "What pang
> Is permanent with man? From the highest,
> As from the vilest thing of every day
> He learns to wean himself. For the strong hours
> Conquer him." [13]

[13] *Death of Wallenstein*, Act v. Scene 1, (Coleridge's Translation,) relating to his remembrances of the younger Piccolomini.

Yes, *there* lies the fountain of human oblivions. It is TIME, the great conqueror, it is the "strong hours" whose batteries storm every passion of men. For, in the fine expression of Schiller, "*Was verschmerzte nicht der mensch?*" What sorrow is in man that will not finally fret itself to sleep? Conquering, at last, gates of brass, or pyramids of granite, why should it be a marvel to us, or a triumph to Time, that he is able to conquer a frail human heart?

However, for this once, my cynic must submit to be told that he is wrong. Doubtless, it is presumption in me to suggest that his sneers can ever go awry, anymore than the shafts of Apollo. But still, however Impossible such a thing is, in this one case it happens that they *have*. And when it happens that they do not, I will tell you, reader, why, in my opinion, it is; and you will see that it warrants no exultation in the cynic. Repeatedly I have heard a mother reproaching herself, when the birth-day revolved of the little daughter whom so suddenly she had lost, with her own insensibility, that could so soon need a remembrancer of the day. But, besides that the majority of people in this world (as being people called to labor) have no time left for cherishing grief by solitude and meditation, always it is proper to ask whether the memory of the lost person were chiefly dependent upon a visual image. No death is usually half so affecting as the death of a young child from two to five years old.

But yet, for the same reason which makes the grief more exquisite, generally for such a loss it is likely to be more perishable. Wherever the image, visually or audibly, of the lost person, is more essential to the life of the grief, there the grief will be more transitory.

Faces begin soon (in Shakspeare's fine expression) to "dislimn;" features fluctuate; combinations of feature unsettle. Even the expression becomes a mere idea that you can describe to another, but not an image. that you can reproduce for yourself. Therefore it is that the faces of infants, though they are divine as flowers in a savanna of Texas, or as the carolling of birds in a forest, are, like flowers in Texas, and the carolling of birds in a forest, soon overtaken by the pursuing darkness that swallows up all things human. All glories of flesh vanish; and this, the glory of infantine beauty seen in the mirror of the memory, soonest of all. But when the departed persons worked upon yourself by powers that were intellectual and moral powers in the flesh, though not of the flesh, -the memorials in your own heart become more steadfast, if less affecting at the first. Now, in my sister were combined for me both graces,—the graces of childhood, and the graces of expanding thought. Besides that, as regards merely the *personal* image, always the smooth rotundity of baby features must vanish sooner, as being less individual than the features in a child of eight, touched with a pensive tenderness, and exalted into a characteristic expression by a premature intellect.

Rarely do things perish from my memory that are worth remembering. Rubbish dies instantly. Hence it happens that passages in Latin or English poets, which I never could have read but once (and *that* thirty years ago), often begin to blossom anew when I am lying awake, unable to sleep. I become a distinguished compositor in the darkness: and, with my aerial composing-stick, sometimes I "set up" half a page of verses, that would be found tolerably correct if collated with the volume that I never had in my hand but once. I mention this in no spirit of boasting. Far from it: for, on the contrary, among my mortifications have been compliments to my memory, when, in fact, any compliment that I had merited was due to the higher faculty of an electric aptitude for seizing analogies, and by means of those aerial pontoons passing over like lightning from one topic to another. Still it is a fact that this pertinacious life of memory for things that simply touch the ear, without touching the consciousness, does, in fact, beset me. Said but once, said but softly, not marked at all, words revive before me in darkness and solitude; and they arrange themselves gradually into sentences, but through an effort some times of a distressing kind, to which I am in a manner forced to become a party. This being so, it was no great instance of that power, that three separate passages in the funeral service, all of which but one had escaped my notice at the time, and even that one as to the part I am going to mention, but all of which must have struck on my ear, restored themselves perfectly when I was lying awake in bed; and though struck by their beauty, I was also incensed by what seemed to me the harsh sentiment expressed in two of these passages. I will cite all the three in an abbreviated form, both for my immediate purpose, and for the indirect purpose of giving to those unacquainted with the English funeral service some specimens of its beauty.

The first passage was this: "Forasmuch as it hath pleased Almighty God, of his great mercy, to take unto. himself the soul of our dear sister here departed, we therefore commit her body to the ground, earth to earth,. ashes to ashes. dust to dust, in sure and certain hope of the resurrection to eternal life." * * *

I pause to remark that a sublime effect arises at this point through a sudden rapturous interpolation from the Apocalypse, which, according to the rubric, "shall be said or sung;" but always let it be sung, and by the full choir:—

"I heard a voice from heaven saying unto me, Write, from henceforth blessed are the dead which die in the Lord; even so saith the Spirit; for they rest from their labors."

The second passage, almost immediately succeeding to this awful burst of heavenly trumpets, and the one which more particularly offended me, though otherwise even then, in my seventh year, I could not but be touched by its beauty, was this:—

"Almighty. God, with whom do live the spirits of them that depart hence in the Lord, and with whom the souls of the faithful, after they are delivered from the burden of the flesh, are in joy and felicity; WE give thee-hearty thanks that it hath pleased thee to deliver this our sister out of the miseries of this sinful world; beseeching thee, that it may please thee of thy gracious goodness shortly to accomplish the number of thine elect, and to hasten thy kingdom." * * *

In what world was I living when a man (calling himself a man of God) could stand up publicly and give God "hearty thanks" that he had taken away any sister? But, young child, understand - taken her away from the miseries of this sinful world. O yes! I hear what you say; I understand *that*; but that makes no difference at all. She being gone, this world doubtless (as you say) is a world of unhappiness. But for me *ubi Caesar, ibi Roma* —where my sister was, there was paradise; no matter whether in heaven above, or on the earth beneath. And he had taken her away, cruel priest! of his "*great* mercy!" I did not presume, child though I was, to think rebelliously against *that*. The reason was not any hypocritical or canting submission where my heart yielded none, but because already my deep musing intellect had perceived a mystery and a labyrinth in the economies of this world. God, I saw, moved not as *we* moved— walked not as *we* walked—thought not as *we* think. Still I saw no mercy to myself, a poor, frail, dependent creature, torn away so suddenly from the prop on which altogether it depended. O yes! perhaps there was; and many years after I came to suspect it. Nevertheless it was a benignity that pointed far ahead; such as by a child could not have been perceived, because then the great arch had not come round; could not have been recognized, if it *had* come round; could not have been valued, if it had even been dimly recognized.

Finally, as the closing prayer in the whole service, stood this, which I acknowledged then, and now acknowledge, as equally beautiful and consolatory; for in this was no harsh peremptory challenge to the infirmities of human grief, as to a thing not meriting notice in a religious rite. On the contrary, there was a gracious condescension from the great apostle to grief, as to a passion that he might perhaps himself have participated.

"O, merciful God! the Father of our Lord Jesus Christ, who is the resurrection and the life, in whom whosoever believeth shall live, though he die; who also taught us by his holy apostle St. Paul not to be sorry, as men without hope, for them that sleep in him; we meekly beseech thee, oh Father! to raise us from the death of sin unto the life of righteousness; that, when we shall depart this life, we may rest in *him* as our hope is- that this our sister doth."

Ah, *that* was beautiful,—that was heavenly! We might be sorry, we had leave to be sorry; only not without hope. And we were by hope to rest in *Him*, as this our sister doth. And howsoever a man may think that he is without hope, I, that have read the writing upon these great abysses of grief, and viewed their shadows under the correction of mightier shadows from deeper abysses since then, abysses of aboriginal fear and eldest darkness, in which yet I believe that all hope had not absolutely died, know that he is in a natural error. If, for a moment, 1 and so many others, wallowing in the dust of affliction, could yet rise up suddenly like the dry corpse [14] which stood upright in the glory of life when touched by the bones of the prophet; if in those vast choral anthems, heard by my childish ear, the voice of God wrapt itself as in a cloud of music, saying—"Child, that sorrowest, I command thee to rise up and ascend for a season into my heaven of heavens,"—then it was plain that despair, that the anguish of darkness, was not *essential* to such sorrow, but might come and go even as light comes and goes upon our troubled earth.

[14] "*Like the dry corpse which stood upright.*"—see the *Second* Book of Kings, chap. xiii. v. 20 and 21. Thirty years ago this impressive incident was made the subject of a large altar-piece by Mr Alston, an interesting American artist, then resident in London.

Yes! the light may come and go; grief may wax and wane; grief may sink; and grief again may rise, as in impassioned minds oftentimes it does, even to the heaven of heavens; but there is a necessity that, if too much left to itself in solitude, finally it will descend into a depth from which there is no re-ascent; into a disease which seems no disease; into a languishing which, from its very sweetness, perplexes the mind, and.. is fancied to be very health. Witchcraft has seized upon you, nympholepsy has struck you. Now you rave no more. You acquiesce; nay, you are passionately delighted in your condition. Sweet becomes the grave, because you also hope immediately to travel thither: luxurious is the separation, because only perhaps for a few weeks shall it exist for you; and it will then prove but the brief summer night that had retarded a little, by a refinement of rapture, the heavenly dawn of reunion. Inevitable sometimes it is in solitude—that this should happen with minds morbidly meditative; that, when we stretch out our arms in darkness, vainly striving to draw back the sweet faces that have vanished, slowly arises a new stratagem of grief, and we say," Be it that they no more come back to us, yet what hinders but we should go to *them?*"

Perilous is that crisis for the young. In its effect perfectly the same as the ignoble witchcraft of the poor African *Obeah* [15] , this sublimer witchcraft of grief will, if left to follow its own natural course, terminate in the same catastrophe of death. Poetry, which neglects no phenomena that are interesting to the heart of man, has sometimes touched a little

"On the sublime attractions of the grave."

[15] "*African Obeah.*" Thirty years ago it would not have been necessary to say one word of the Obi or Obeah magic; because at that time several distinguished writers (Miss Edgeworth, for instance, in her Belinda) had made use of this superstition in fictions, and because the remarkable history of Three-finger'd Jack, a story brought upon the stage, had made the superstition notorious as a fact. Now, however, so long after the case has probably passed out of the public mind, it may be proper to mention—that when an Obeah mind, *i.e.*, a professor of this dark collusion with human fears and human credulity, had once woven his dreadful net of ghostly terrors, and had thrown it over his selected victim, vainly id that victim flutter, struggle, languish in the meshes; unless the spells were reversed, he generally perished; and without a wound except from his own too domineering fancy.

But you think that these attractions, existing at times for the adult, could not exist for the child. Understand that you are wrong. Understand that these attractions *do* exist for the child; and perhaps as much more strongly than they *can* exist for the adult, by the whole difference between the concentration of a childish love, and the inevitable distraction upon multiplied objects of any love that can affect any adult. There is a German superstition (well known by a popular translation) of the Erl-king's Daughter, who fixes her love upon some child, and seeks to wile him away into her own shadowy kingdom in forests.

"Who is it that rides through the forest so fast?"

It is a knight, who carries his child before him on the saddle. The Erl-king's Daughter rides on his right hand, and still whispers temptations to the infant audible only to *him*.

"If thou wilt, dear baby, with me go away,
We will see a fine show, we will play a fine play."

The consent of the baby is essential to her success. And finally she *does* succeed. Other charms, other temptations, would have been requisite for me. My intellect was too advanced for those fascinations. But could the Erl-king's Daughter have revealed herself to me, and promised to lead me where my sister was, she might have wiled me by the hand into the dimmest forests upon earth. Languishing was my condition at that time. Still I languished for things "which" (a voice from heaven seemed to answer through my own heart) "*cannot* be granted;" and which, when again I languished, again the voice repeated, "*cannot* be granted."

Well it was for me that, at this crisis, I was summoned to put on the harness of life by commencing my classical studies under one of my guardians, a clergyman. of the English Church, and (so far as regarded Latin) a most accomplished scholar.

At the very commencement of my new studies there happened an incident which afflicted me much for a short time, and left behind a gloomy impression, that suffering and wretchedness were diffused amongst all creatures that breathe. A person had given me a kitten. There are three animals which seem, beyond all others, to reflect the beauty of human infancy in two of its elements—namely, joy and guileless innocence, though less in its third element of simplicity, because *that* requires language for its full expression: these three animals are the kitten, the lamb, and the fawn. Other creatures may be as happy, but they do not show it so much. Great was the love which poor silly I had for this little kitten; but, as I left home at ten in the morning, and did not return till near five in the afternoon, I was obliged, with some anxiety, to throw it for those seven hours upon its own discretion, as infirm a basis for reasonable hope as could be imagined. I did not wish the kitten, indeed, at all less foolish than it was, except just when I was leaving home, and then its exceeding folly gave me a pang. Just about that time, it happened that we had received, as a present from Leicestershire, a fine young Newfoundland dog, who was under a cloud of disgrace for crimes of his youthful blood committed in that county. One day he had taken too great a liberty with a pretty little cousin of mine, Emma H, about four years old. He had, in fact, bitten off her cheek, which, remaining attached by a shred, vas, through the energy of a governess, replaced, and subsequently healed without a scar. His name being *Turk*, he was immediately pronounced by the best Greek scholar of that neighborhood, επωνυος (*i.e.*, named significantly, or reporting his nature in his name). But as Miss Emma confessed to having been engaged in taking away a bone from him, on which subject no dog can be taught to understand a joke, it did not strike our own authorities that he was to be considered in a state of reprobation; and as our gardens (near to a great town) were, on account chiefly of melons, constantly robbed, it was held that a moderate degree of fierceness was rather a favorable trait in his character. My poor kitten, it was supposed, had been engaged in the same playful trespass upon Turk's property as my Leicestershire cousin, and Turk laid her dead on the spot. It is impossible to describe my grief when the case was made known to me at five o'clock in the evening, by a man's holding out the little creature dead: she that I had left so full of glorious life,—life which even in a kitten is infinite,—was now stretched in motionless repose. I remember that there was a large coal-stack in the yard. I dropped my Latin books, sat down upon a huge block of coal, and burst into a passion of tears. The man, struck with my tumultuous grief, hurried into the house; and from the lower regions deployed instantly the women of the laundry and the kitchen. No one subject is so absolutely sacred, and enjoys so classical a sanctity among servant-girls, as 1. Grief; and 2. Love which is unfortunate. All the young women took me up in their arms and kissed me; and, last of all, an elderly woman, who was the cook, not only kissed me, but wept so audibly, from some suggestion doubtless of grief personal to herself, that I threw my arms about her neck and kissed *her* also. It is probable, as I now suppose, that some account of my grief for my sister had reached them. Else I was never allowed to visit *their* region of the house. But, however *that* might be, afterwards it struck me, that if I had met with so much sympathy, or with any sympathy at all, from the servant chiefly connected with myself in the desolating grief I had suffered, possibly I should not have been so profoundly shaken.

But did I in the mean time feel anger towards Turk? Not the least. And the reason was this:—My guardian, who taught me Latin, was in the habit of coming over and dining at my mother's table whenever he pleased. On these occasions, he, who like myself pitied *dependent* animals, went invariably into the yard of the offices, taking me with him, and unchained the dogs. There were two,—Grim , a mastiff, and *Turk*, our young friend. My guardian was a bold, athletic man, and delighted in dogs. He told me, which also my own heart told me, that these poor dogs languished out their lives under this confinement. The moment that I and my guardian (*ego et rex meus*) appeared in sight of the two kennels, it is impossible to express the joy of the dogs. Turk was usually restless; Grim slept away his life in surliness. But at the sight of us,—of my little insignificant self and my six-foot guardian,—both dogs yelled with delight. We unfastened their chains with our own hands, they licking our hands; and as to myself, licking my miserable little face; and at one bound they reentered upon their natural heritage of joy. Always we took them through the fields, where they molested nothing, and closed with giving them a cold bath in the brook which bounded my father's property. What despair must have possessed our dogs when they were taken back to their hateful prisons! and I, for my part, not enduring to see their misery, slunk away when the rechaining commenced. It was in vain to tell me that all people, who had property out of doors to protect, chained up dogs in the same way; *this* only proved the extent of the oppression; for a monstrous oppression it *did* seem, that creatures, boiling with life and the desires of life, should be thus detained in captivity until they were set free by death. That liberation visited poor *Grim* and *Turk* sooner than any of us expected, for they were both poisoned, within the year that followed, by a party of burglars. At the end of that year, I was reading the Æneid; and it struck me, who remembered the howling recusancy of *Turk*, as a peculiarly fine circumstance, introduced amongst the horrors of Tartarus, that sudden gleam of powerful animals, full of life and conscious rights, rebelling against chains:—

"Iraeque leonum
Vincla recusantum." [16]

[16] What follows, I think, (for book I have none of any kind where this paper is proceeding,) viz. *et sera sub nocte rudentum*, is probably a mistake of Virgil's; the lions did not roar because night was approaching, but because night brought with it their principal meal, and consequently the impatience of hunger.

Virgil had doubtless picked up that gem in his visits at feeding-time to the *caveae* of the Roman amphitheatre. But the rights of brute creatures to a merciful forbearance on the part of man could not enter into the feeblest conceptions of one belonging to a nation that (although too noble to be *wantonly* cruel) yet in the same amphitheatre manifested so little regard even to human rights. Under Christianity the condition of the brute has improved, and will improve much more. There is ample room. For, I am sorry to say, that the commonest vice of Christian children, too often surveyed with careless eyes by mothers that in their *human* relations are full of kindness, is cruelty to the inferior creatures thrown upon their mercy. For my own part, what had formed the ground-work of my happiness (since joyous was my nature, though overspread with a cloud of sadness) had been from the first a heart overflowing with love. And I had drunk in too profoundly the spirit of Christianity from our many nursery readings, not to read also in its divine words the justification of my own tendencies. That which I desired was the thing which I ought to desire; the mercy that I loved was the mercy that God had blessed. From the Sermon on the Mount resounded forever in my ears "Blessed are the merciful!" I needed not to add—" For they shall obtain mercy." By lips so holy, and when standing in the atmosphere of truths so divine, simply to have been blessed—*that* was a sufficient ratification; every truth so revealed, and so hallowed by. position, starts into sudden life, and becomes to itself its own authentication, needing no proof to convince,—needing no promise to allure.

It may well be supposed, therefore, that having so early awakened within me what may be philosophically called the *transcendental* justice of Christianity, I blamed not *Turk* for yielding to the coercion of his nature. He had killed the object of my love. But, besides that he was under the constraint of a primary appetite, Turk was himself the victim of a killing oppression. He was doomed to a fretful existence so long as he should exist at all. Nothing could reconcile this to my benignity, which at that time rested upon two pillars,—upon the deep, deep heart which God had given to me at my birth, and upon exquisite health. Up to the age of two, and almost through that entire space of twenty-four months, I had suffered from ague; but when *that* left me, all germs and traces of ill health fled away forever, except only such (and those how curable!) as I inherited from my school-boy distresses in London, or had created by means of opium. Even the long ague was not without ministrations of favor to my prevailing temper; and, on the whole, no subject for pity, since naturally it won for me the sweet caresses of female tenderness, both young and old. I was a little petted; but you see by this time, reader, that I must have been too much of a philosopher, even in the year one *ab urbe condita* of my frail earthly tenement, to abuse such indulgence. It also won for me a ride on horseback whenever the weather permitted. I was placed on a pillow, in front of a cankered old man, upon a large white horse, not so young as I was, but still showing traces of blood. And even the old man, who was both the oldest and the worst of the three, talked with gentleness to myself, reserving his surliness for all the rest of the world.

These things pressed with a gracious power of incubation upon my predispositions; and in my overflowing love I did things fitted to make the reader laugh, and sometimes fitted to bring myself into perplexity. One instance from a thousand may illustrate the combination of both effects. At four years old, I had repeatedly seen the housemaid raising her long, broom, and pursuing (generally destroying) a vagrant spider. The holiness of all life, in my eyes, forced me to devise plots for saving the poor doomed wretch; and thinking intercession likely to prove useless, my policy was, to draw off the housemaid on pretence of showing her a picture, until the spider, already en route, should have had time to escape. Very soon, however, the shrewd housemaid, marking the coincidence of these picture exhibitions with the agonies of fugitive spiders, detected my stratagem; so that, if the reader will pardon an expression borrowed from the street, henceforwards the picture was "no go." However, as she approved of my motive, she told me of the many murders that the spider had committed, and next (which was worse) of the many that he certainly *would* commit, if reprieved. This staggered me. I could have gladly forgiven the past; but it did seem a false mercy to spare one spider in order to scatter death amongst fifty flies. I thought timidly, for a moment, of suggesting that people sometimes repented, and that *he* might repent; but I checked myself, on-considering that I had never read any account, and that she might laugh at the idea, of a penitent spider. To desist was a necessity, in these circumstances. But the difficulty which the housemaid had suggested did not depart; it troubled my musing mind to perceive that the welfare of one creature might stand upon the ruin of another; and the case of the spider remained thenceforwards even more perplexing to my understanding than it was painful to my heart.

The reader is likely to differ from me upon the question, moved by recurring to such experiences of childhood, whether much value attaches to the perceptions and intellectual glimpses of a child. Children, like men, range through a gamut that is infinite, of temperaments and characters, ascending from the very dust below our feet to highest heaven. I have seen children that were sensual, brutal, devilish. But, thanks be to the *vis medicatrix* of human nature, and to the goodness of God, these are as rare exhibitions as all other monsters. People thought, when seeing such odious travesties and burlesques upon lovely human infancy, that perhaps the little wretches might be *kilcrops* [17].Yet, possibly (it has since occurred to me), even these children of the fiend, as they seemed, might have one chord in their horrible natures that answered to the call of some sublime purpose. There is a mimic instance of this kind, often found amongst ourselves in natures that are not really " horrible," but which *seem* such to persons viewing them from a station not sufficiently central:—Always there are mischievous boys in a neighborhood,—boys who tie canisters to the tails of cats belonging to ladies,—a thing which *greatly* I disapprove; and who rob orchards,—a thing which *slightly* I disapprove; and, behold! the next day, on meeting the injured ladies, they say to me, "O, my dear friend, never pretend to argue for him! This boy, we shall all see, will come to be hanged." Well, that seems a disagreeable prospect for all parties; so I change the subject; and, lo! five years later, there is an English frigate fighting with a frigate of heavier metal (no matter of what nation). The noble captain has maneuvered as only his countrymen can maneuver; he has delivered his broadsides as only the proud islanders can deliver them. Suddenly he sees the opening for a *coup-de-main*; through his speaking-trumpet he shouts, "*Where are my boarders?*" And instantly rise upon the deck, with the gayety of boyhood, in white shirt-sleeves bound with black ribbons, fifty men, the *élite* of the crew; and, behold! at the very head of them, cutlass in hand, is our-friend, the tier of canisters to the tails of ladies' cats,—a thing which *greatly* I disapprove, and also the robber of orchards,—a thing which *slightly* I disapprove. But here is a man that will not suffer you either greatly or slightly to disapprove him. Fire celestial burns in his eye; his nation—his glorious nation—is in his mind; himself he regards no more than the life of a cat, or the ruin of a canister. On the deck of the enemy he throws himself with rapture; and if *he* is amongst the killed,—if he, for an object so gloriously unselfish, lays down with joy his life and glittering youth,—mark this, that, perhaps, he will not be the least in heaven.

But coming back to the case of childhood, I maintain steadfastly that into all the *elementary* feelings of man children look with more searching gaze than adults. My opinion is, that where circumstances favor, where the heart is deep, where humility and tenderness exist in strength, where the situation is favorable as to solitude and as to genial feelings, children have a specific power of contemplating the truth, which departs as they enter the world. It is clear to me, that children, upon elementary paths which require no knowledge of the world to unravel, tread more firmly than men; have a more pathetic sense of the beauty which lies in justice; and, according to the immortal ode of our great laureate [ode "On the Intimations of Immortality in Childhood"], a far closer communion with God. I, if you observe, do not much intermeddle with religion, properly so called. My path lies on the interspace between religion and philosophy, that connects them both. Yet here, for once, I shall trespass on grounds not properly mine, and desire you to observe in St. Matthew, chapter xxi., and verse 15, who were those that, crying in the temple, made the first public recognition of Christianity. Then, if you say, "O, but children echo what they hear, and are no independent authorities!" I must request you to extend your reading into verse 16, where you will find that the testimony of these children, as bearing an *original* value, was ratified by the highest testimony; and the recognition of these children did itself receive a heavenly recognition. And this could *not* have been, unless there were children in Jerusalem who saw into truth with a far sharper eye than Sanhedrims and Rabbis.

It is impossible, with respect to any memorable grief, that it can be adequately exhibited so as to indicate the enormity of the convulsion which really it caused, without viewing it under a variety of aspects,- a thing which is here almost necessary for the effect of proportion to what follows: 1st, for instance, in its immediate pressure, so stunning and confounding; 2dly, in its oscillations, as in its earlier agitations, frantic with tumults, that borrow the wings of the winds; or in its diseased impulses of sick languishing desire, through which sorrow transforms itself to a sunny angel, that beckons us to a sweet repose. These phases of revolving affection I have already sketched. And I shall. also sketch a third, that is, where the affliction, seemingly hushing itself to sleep, suddenly soars upwards, again upon combining with *another* mode of sorrow, namely, anxiety without definite limits, and the trouble of a reproaching conscience. As sometimes [18], upon the English lakes, water-fowl that have careered in the air until the eye is wearied with the eternal wheelings of their inimitable flight— Grecian simplicities of motion, amidst a labyrinthine infinity of curves that would baffle the geometry of Apollonius—seek the water at last, as if with some settled purpose (you imagine) of reposing. Ah, how little have you understood the omnipotence of that life which they inherit! *They* want no rest: they laugh at resting; all is "make believe," as when an infant hides its laughing face behind its mother's shawl. For a moment it is still. Is it meaning to rest? Will its impatient heart endure to lurk there for long? Ask, rather, if a cataract will stop from fatigue. Will a sunbeam sleep on its travels? or the Atlantic rest from its labors? As little can the infant, as little can the water-fowl of the lakes, suspend their play, except as a variety of play, or rest unless. when nature compels them, Suddenly starts off the infant, suddenly ascend the birds, to new evolutions as incalculable as the caprices of a kaleidoscope; and the glory of their motions, from the mixed immortalities of beauty and inexhaustible variety, becomes at least pathetic to survey. So also, and with such life of variation, do the primary convulsions of nature—such, perhaps, as only *primary* [19] formations in the human system can experience—come round again and again by reverberating shocks.

[18] In this place I derive my feeling partly from a lovely sketch of the appearance, in verse, by Mr Wordsworth; partly from my own experience of the case; and, not having the poems here, I know not how to proportion my acknowledgments.
[19] "And so, then," the Cynic objects, "you rank your own mind (and you tell us so frankly) amongst the primary formations?" As I love to annoy him, it would give me pleasure to reply—"Perhaps I do." But as I never answer more questions than are necessary, I confine myself to saying, that this is not a necessary construction of the words. Some minds stand nearer to the type of the original nature in man, are truer than others to the great magnet in our dark planet. Minds that are impassioned on a more colossal scale than ordinary, deeper in their vibrations, and more extensive in the scale of their vibrations—whether, in other parts of their intellectual system, they had not had a corresponding compass—will tremble to greater depths from a fearful convulsion, and will come round by a longer curve of undulations.

The new intercourse with my guardian, and the changes of scene which naturally it led to, were of use in weaning my mind from the mere disease which threatened it in case I had been left any longer to my total solitude. But out of these changes grew an incident which restored my grief, though in a more troubled shape, and now—for the first time associated with something like remorse and deadly anxiety. I can safely say that this was my earliest trespass, and perhaps a venial one, all things considered. Nobody ever discovered it; and but for my own frankness it would not be known to this day. But *that* I could not know; and for years,—that is, from seven or earlier up to ten,—such was my simplicity, that I lived in constant terror. This, though it revived my grief, did me probably great service; because it was no longer a state of languishing desire tending to torpor, but of feverish irritation and gnawing care, that kept alive the activity of my understanding. The case was this:—It happened that I had now, and commencing with my first introduction to Latin studies, a large weekly allowance of pocket-money,—too large for my age, but safely entrusted to myself, who never spent or desired to spend one fraction of it upon anything but books. But all proved too little for my colossal schemes. Had the Vatican, the Bodleian, and the *Bibliothèque du Roi*, been all emptied into one collection for my private gratification, little progress would have been made towards content in this particular craving. Very soon I had run ahead of my allowance, and was about three guineas deep in debt. There I paused; for deep anxiety now began to oppress me as to the course in which this mysterious (and indeed guilty) current of debt would finally flow. For the present it was frozen up; but I had some reason for thinking that Christmas thawed all debts whatsoever, and set them in motion towards innumerable pockets. Now my debt would be thawed with all the rest; and in what direction would it flow? There was no river that would carry it off to sea; to somebody's pocket it would beyond a doubt make its way; and who was that somebody? This question haunted me forever. Christmas had come, Christmas had gone, and I heard nothing of the three guineas. But I was not easier for *that*. Far rather I would have heard of it; for this indefinite approach of a loitering catastrophe gnawed and fretted my feelings. No Grecian audience ever waited with more shuddering horror for the anagnorisis [20] of the Œdipus, who could not possibly care for my trifling custom than I for the explosion of my debt. Had I been less ignorant, I should have proposed to mortgage my weekly allowance for the debt, or to form a sinking fund for redeeming it; for the *weekly* sum was nearly five per cent. on the entire debt. But I had a mysterious awe of ever alluding to it. This arose from my want of some confidential friend; whilst my grief pointed continually to the remembrance, that so it had not always been. But was not the bookseller to blame in suffering a child scarcely seven years old to contract such a debt? Not in the least. He was both a rich man, and notoriously an honorable man. Indeed, the money which I myself spent every week in books would reasonably have caused him to presume that so small a sum as three guineas might well be authorized by my family. He stood, however, on plainer ground; for my guardian, who was very indolent (as people chose to call it),—that is, like his little melancholy ward, spent all his time in reading,—often enough would send me to the bookseller's with a written order for books. This was to prevent my forgetting. But when he found that such a thing as "forgetting," in the case of a book, was wholly out of the question for me, the trouble of writing was dismissed. And thus I had become factor-general, on the part of my guardian, both for *his* books, and for such as were wanted on my own account, in the natural course of my education. My private "little. account" had therefore in fact flowed homewards at Christmas, not (as I anticipated) in the shape of an independent current, but as a little tributary rill, that was lost in the waters of some more important river. This I now know, but could not then have known with any certainty. So far, however, the affair would gradually have sunk out of my anxieties, as time wore on. But there was another item in the case, which, from the excess of my ignorance, preyed upon my spirits far more keenly; and this, keeping itself alive, kept also the other incident alive. With respect to the debt, I was not so ignorant as to think it of much danger by the mere amount,—my own allowance furnished a scale for preventing *that* mistake;—it was the principle,—the having presumed to contract debts on my own account,—that I feared to have exposed. But this other case was a ground for anxiety, even as regarded the amount; not really, but under the jesting representation made to me, which I (as ever before and after) swallowed in perfect faith. Amongst the books which I had bought, all English, was a history of Great Britain, commencing, of course, with Brutus and a thousand years of impossibilities; these fables being generously thrown in as a little gratuitous extra to the mass of truths which were to follow. This was to be completed in sixty or eighty parts, I believe. But there was another work left more indefinite as to its ultimate extent, and' which, from its nature, seemed to imply a far higher range. It was a general history of navigation, supported by a vast body of voyages. Now, when I considered with myself what a huge thing the sea was, and that so many thousands of captains, commodores, admirals, were eternally running up and down it, and scoring lines upon its face so rankly, that in some of the main "streets" and "squares" (as one might call them), their tracts would blend into one undistinguishable blot, I began to fear that such a work tended to infinity. What was little England to the universal sea? And yet that went perhaps to fourscore parts. Not enduring the uncertainty that now besieged my tranquillity, I resolved to know the worst; and, on a day ever memorable to me, I went down to the bookseller's. He was a mild, elderly man, and to myself had always shown a kind, indulgent manner. Partly, perhaps, he had been struck by my extreme gravity; and partly, during the many conversations I had with him, on occasion of my guardian's orders for books, with my laughable simplicity. But there was another reason which had early won for me his paternal regard. For the first three or four months I had found Latin something of a drudgery; and the incident which forever knocked away the "shores," at that time preventing my launch upon the general bosom of Latin literature, was this:- One day, the bookseller took down a Beza's *Latin Testament*; and, opening it, asked me to translate for him the chapter which he pointed to. I was struck by perceiving that it was the great chapter of St. Paul on the grave and resurrection. I had never seen a Latin version; yet, from the simplicity of the scriptural style in *any* translation (though Beza's is far from good), I could not well have failed in construing. But, as it happened to be this particular chapter, which in English I had read again and again with so passionate a sense of its grandeur, I read it off with a fluency and effect like some great opera singer uttering a rapturous *bravura*. My kind old friend expressed himself gratified, making me a present of the book as a mark of his approbation. And it is remarkable, that from this moment, when the deep memory of the English words had forced me into seeing the precise correspondence of the two concurrent streams,—Latin and English,— never again did any difficulty arise to check the velocity of my progress in this particular language. At less than eleven years of age, when as yet I was a very indifferent Grecian, I had become a brilliant master of Latinity, as my Alcaics and Choriambics remain to testify; and the whole occasion of a change so memorable to a boy, was this casual summons to translate a composition with which my heart was filled. Ever after this, he showed me a caressing kindness, and so condescendingly, that, generally, he would leave any people, for a moment, with whom he was engaged, to come and speak to me. On this fatal day, however, for such it proved to me,—he could not do this. He saw me, indeed, and nodded, but could not leave a party of elderly strangers. This accident threw me unavoidably upon one of his young people. Now, this was a market day, and there was a press of country people present, whom I did not wish to hear my question. Never did a human creature, with his heart palpitating at Delphi for the solution of some killing mystery, stand before the priestess of the oracle, with lips that moved more sadly than mine, when now advancing to a smiling young man at a desk. His answer was to decide, though I could not exactly know *that*, whether, for the next two years, I was to have an hour of peace. He was a handsome, good-natured young man, but full of fun and frolic; and I dare say was amused with what must have seem to *him* the absurd anxiety of my features. I described the work to him, and he understood me at once. How many volumes did he think it would extend to? There was a whimsical expression, perhaps, of drollery about his eyes, but which, unhappily, under my preconceptions, I translated into scorn, as he replied, "How many volumes? O! really, I can't say; maybe a matter of 15,000, be the same more or less." "*More?*" I said, in horror, altogether neglecting the contingency of "less." "Why," he said, "we can't settle these things to a nicety. But, considering the subject" [ay, *that* was the very thing which I myself considered], "I should say there might be some trifle over, as suppose 400 or 500 volumes, be the same more or less." What, then,— here there might be supplements to supplements,—the work might positively never end! On one pretence or another, if an author or publisher might add 500 volumes, he might add another round 15,000.' Indeed, it strikes one even now, that by the time all the one-legged commodores and yellow admirals of that generation had exhausted their long yarns, another generation would have grown another crop of the same gallant spinners. I asked no more, but slunk out of the shop, and never again entered it with cheerfulness, or propounded any frank questions, as heretofore. For I was now seriously afraid of pointing attention to myself as one that, by having purchased some numbers, and obtained others on credit, had silently contracted an engagement to take all the rest, though they should stretch to the crack of doom. Certainly I had never heard of a work that extended to 15,000 volumes; but still there was no natural impossibility that it should; and, if in any case, in none so reasonably as one upon the inexhaustible sea. Besides, any slight mistake as to the letter of the number could not affect the horror of the final prospect. I saw by the imprint, and I heard, that this work emanated from London, a vast centre of mystery to me, and the more so, as a thing unseen at any time by my eyes, and nearly two hundred miles distant. I felt the fatal truth, that here was a ghostly cobweb radiating into all the provinces from the mighty metropolis. I secretly had trodden upon the outer circumference, had damaged or deranged the fine threads or links, concealment or reparation there could be none. Slowly perhaps, but surely, the vibration would travel back to London. The ancient spider that sat there at the centre would rush along the net-work through all longitudes and latitudes, until he found the responsible caitiff, author of so much mischief. Even with less ignorance than mine, there *was* something to appal a child's imagination in the vast systematic machinery by which any elaborate work could disperse itself, could levy money, could put questions and get answers, all in profound silence, nay, even in darkness, searching every nook of every town and of every hamlet in so populous a kingdom. I had some dim terrors, also, connected with the Stationers' Company. I had often observed them in popular works threatening unknown men with unknown chastisements, for offences equally unknown; nay, to myself, absolutely inconceivable. Could *I* be the mysterious criminal so long pointed out, as it were, in prophecy? I figured the stationers, doubtless all powerful men, pulling at one rope, and my unhappy self hanging at the other end. But an image, which seems now even more ludicrous than the rest, at that time, was the one most connected with the revival of my grief. It occurred to my subtlety, that the Stationers' Company, or any other company, could not possibly demand the money until they had delivered the volumes. Ant, as no man could say that I had ever positively refused to receive them, they would have no pretence for not accomplishing this delivery in a civil manner. Unless I should turn out to be no customer at all, at present it was clear that I had a right to be considered a most excellent customer; one, in fact, who had given an order for fifteen thousand volumes. Then rose up before me this great opera-house "scena" of the delivery. There would be a ring at the front door. A wagoner in the front, with a bland voice, would ask for "a young gentleman who had given an order to their house." Looking out, I should perceive a procession of carts and wagons, all advancing in measured movements; each in turn would present its rear, deliver its cargo of volumes, by shooting them, like a load of coals, on the lawn, and wheel off to the rear, by way of clearing the road for its successors. Then the impossibility of even asking the servants to cover with sheets, or counterpanes, or table-cloths, such a mountainous, such a " star-y-pointing " record of my past offences, lying in so conspicuous a situation! Men would not know my guilt merely, they would see it. But the reason why this form of the consequences, so much more than any other, stuck by my imagination was, that it connected itself with one of the Arabian Nights which had particularly interested myself and my sister. It was that tale, where a young porter, having his ropes about his person, had stumbled into the special "preserve" of some old magician. He finds a beautiful lady imprisoned, to whom (and not without prospects of success) he recommends himself as a suitor more in harmony with her own years than a withered magician. At this crisis, the magician returns. The young man bolts, and for that day successfully; but unluckily he leaves his ropes behind. Next morning he hears the magician, too honest by half, inquiring at the front door, with much expression of condolence, for the unfortunate young man who had lost his ropes' in his own zenana. Upon this story I used to amuse my sister by ventriloquizing to the magician, from the lips of the trembling young man,—" O, Mr. Magician, these ropes cannot be mine! They are far too good; and one would not like, you know, to rob some other poor young man. If you please, Mr. Magician, I never had money enough to buy so beautiful a set of ropes." But argument is thrown away upon a magician, and off he sets on his travels with the young porter, not forgetting to take the ropes along with him.

Here now was the case, that had once seemed so impressive to me in a mere fiction from a far distant age and land, literally reproduced in myself. For, what did it matter whether a magician dunned one with old ropes for his engine of torture, or Stationers' Hall with fifteen thousand volumes (in the rear of which there might also be ropes)? Should I have ventriloquized, would my sister have laughed, had either of us but guessed the possibility that I myself, and within one twelve months, and, alas! standing alone in the world as regarded *confidential* counsel, should repeat within my own inner experience the shadowy panic of the young Bagdat intruder upon the privacy of magicians? It appeared, then, that I had been reading a legend concerning myself in the *Arabian Nights*. I had been contemplated in types a thousand years before, on the banks of the Tigris. It was horror and grief that prompted that thought.

Oh, heavens! that the misery of a child should by possibility become the laughter of adults!—that even I, the sufferer, should be capable of amusing myself, as if it had been a jest, with what for three years had constituted the secret affliction of my life, and its eternal trepidation—like the ticking of a death-watch to patients lying awake in the plague! I durst ask no counsel; there was no one to ask. Possibly my sister could have given me none in a case which neither of us should have understood, and where to seek for information from others would have been at once to betray the whole reason for seeking it. But, if no advice, she would have given me her pity, and the expression of her endless love; and, with the relief of sympathy, that heals for a season all distresses, she would have given me that exquisite luxury—the knowledge that, having parted with my secret, yet also I had not parted with it, since it was in the power only of one that could much less betray me than I could betray myself. At this time,—that is, about the year when I suffered most,— I was reading Caesar. O, laurelled scholar, sun-bright intellect, "foremost man of all this world," how often did I make out of thy immortal volume a pillow to support my wearied brow, as at evening, on my homeward road, I used to turn into some silent field, where I might give way unobserved to the reveries which besieged me! I wondered, and found no end of wondering, at the revolution that one short year had made in my happiness. I wondered that such billows could overtake me. At the beginning of that year, how radiantly happy! At the end, how insupportably alone!

> "Into what depth thou see'st,
> From what height fallen."

Forever I searched the abysses with some wandering thoughts unintelligible to myself. Forever I dallied with some obscure notion, how my sister's love might be made in some dim way available for delivering me from misery; or else how the misery I had suffered and was suffering might be made, in some way equally dim, the ransom for winning back her love.

Here pause, reader! Imagine yourself seated in some cloud-scaling swing, oscillating under the impulse of lunatic hands; for the strength of lunacy may belong to human dreams, the fearful caprice of lunacy, and the malice of lunacy, whilst the *victim* of those dreams may be all the more certainly removed from lunacy; even as a bridge gathers cohesion and strength from the increasing resistance into which it is forced by increasing pressure. Seated in such a swing, fast as you reach the lowest point of depression, may you rely on racing up to a starry altitude of corresponding ascent. Ups and downs you will see, heights and depths, in our fiery course together, such as will sometimes tempt you to look shyly and suspiciously at me, your guide, and the ruler of the oscillations. Here, at the point where I have called a halt, the reader has reached the lowest depths in my nursery afflictions. From that point, according to the principles of art which govern the movement of these Confessions, I had meant to launch him upwards through the whole arch of ascending visions which seemed requisite to balance the sweep downwards, so recently described in his course. But accidents of the press have made it impossible to accomplish this purpose in the present month's journal. There is reason to regret that the advantages of position, which were essential to the full effect of passages planned for the equipoise and mutual resistance, have thus been lost. Meantime, upon the principle of the mariner, who rigs a *jury*-mast in default of his regular spars, I find my resource in a sort of "jury" peroration, not sufficient in the way of a balance by its *proportions*, but sufficient to indicate the *quality* of the balance which I had contemplated. He who has *really* read the preceding parts of these present Confessions will be aware that a stricter scrutiny of the past, such as was natural after the whole economy of the dreaming faculty had been convulsed beyond all precedents on record, led me to the conviction that not one agency, but two agencies, had cooperated to the tremendous result. The nursery experience had been the ally and the natural coefficient of the opium. For that reason it was that the nursery experience has been narrated. Logically it bears the very same relation to the convulsions of the dreaming faculty as the opium. The idealizing tendency existed in the dream-theatre of my childhood; but the preternatural strength of its action and coloring was first developed after the confluence of the two causes. The reader must suppose me at Oxford; twelve years and a half are gone by; I am in the glory of youthful happiness: but I have now first tampered with opium; and now first the agitations of my childhood reopened in strength, now first they swept in upon the brain with power, and the grandeur of recovered life, under the separate and the concurring inspirations of opium.

Once again, after twelve years' interval, the nursery of my childhood expanded before me: my sister was moaning in bed; I was beginning to be restless with fears not intelligible to myself. Once again the nurse, but now dilated to colossal proportions, stood as upon some Grecian stage with her uplifted hand, and, like the superb Medea standing alone with her children in the nursery at Corinth [21], smote me senseless to the ground. Again I was in the chamber with my sister's corpse, again the pomps of life rose up in silence, the glory of summer, the frost of death. Dream formed itself mysteriously within dream; within these Oxford dreams remoulded itself continually the trance in my sister's chamber, the blue heavens, the everlasting vault, the soaring billows, the throne steeped in the thought (but not the sight) of "Him that sate thereon;" the flight, the pursuit, the irrecoverable steps of my return to earth. Once more the funeral procession gathered; the priest in his white surplice stood waiting with a book in his hand by the side of an open grave, the sacristan with his shovel; the coffin sank; the *dust to dust* descended. Again I was in the church on a heavenly Sunday morning. The golden sunlight of God slept amongst the heads of his apostles, his martyrs, his saints; the fragment from the litany, the fragment from the clouds, awoke again the lawny beds that went up to scale the heavens —awoke again the shadowy arms that moved downward to meet them. Once again arose the swell of the anthem, the burst of the Hallelujah chorus, the storm, the trampling movement of the choral passion, the agitation of my own trembling sympathy, the tumult of the choir, the wrath of the organ. Once more 1, that wallowed, became he that rose up to the clouds. And now in Oxford all was bound up into unity; the first state and the last were melted into each other as in some sunny glorifying haze. For high above my own station hovered a gleaming host of heavenly beings, surrounding the pillows of the dying children. And such beings sympathize equally with sorrow that grovels and with sorrow that soars. Such beings pity alike the children that are languishing in death, and the children that live only to languish in tears.

[21] Euripides.

THE PALIMPSEST

You know perhaps, masculine reader, better than I can tell you, what is a *Palimpsest*. Possibly, you have one in your own library. But yet, for the sake of others who may not know, or may have forgotten, suffer me to explain it here, lest any female reader, who honors; these papers with her notice, should tax me with. explaining it once too seldom; which would be worse. to bear than a simultaneous complaint from twelve proud men, that I had explained it three times too often. You therefore, fair reader, understand, that for *your* accommodation exclusively, I explain the meaning of this word. It is Greek; and our sex enjoys the office and privilege of standing counsel to yours, in all questions of Greek. We are, under favor, perpetual and hereditary dragomans to you. So that if, by accident, you know the meaning of a Greek word, yet by courtesy to us, your counsel learned in that matter, you will always seem *not* to know it.

A palimpsest, then, is a membrane or roll cleansed of its manuscript by reiterated successions.

What was the reason that the Greeks and the Romans had not the advantage of printed books? The answer will be, from ninety-nine persons in a hundred,—Because the mystery of printing was not then discovered. But this is altogether a mistake. The secret of printing must have been discovered many thousands of times before it was used, or *could* be used. The inventive powers of man are divine; and also his stupidity is divine, as Cowper so playfully illustrates in the slow development of the *sofa* through successive generations of immortal dullness. It took centuries of blockheads to raise a joint stool into a chair; and it required something like a miracle of genius, in the estimate of elder generations, to reveal the possibility of lengthening a chair into a *chaise-longue*, or a sofa. Yes, these were inventions that cost mighty throes of intellectual power. But still, as respects printing, and admirable as is the stupidity of man, it was really not quite equal to the task of evading an object which stared him in the face with so broad a gaze. It did not require an Athenian intellect to read the main secret of printing in many scores of processes which the ordinary uses of life were *daily* repeating. To say nothing of analogous artifices amongst various mechanic artisans, all that is essential in printing must have been known to every nation that struck coins and medals. Not, therefore, any want. of a printing art,—that is, of an art for multiplying impressions,—but the want of a cheap material for *receiving* such impressions, was the obstacle to an introduction of printed books, even as early as Pisistratus. The ancients *did* apply printing to records of silver and gold; to marble, and many other substances cheaper than gold and silver, they did *not*, since each monument required a separate effort of inscription. Simply this defect it was of a cheap material for receiving impresses, which froze in its very fountains the early resources of printing.

Some twenty years ago, this view of the case was luminously expounded by Dr. Whately, the present Archbishop of Dublin, and with the merit, I believe, of having first suggested it. Since then, this theory has received indirect confirmation. Now, out of that original scarcity affecting all materials proper for durable books, which continued up to times comparatively modern, grew the opening for palimpsests. Naturally, when once a roll of parchment or of vellum had done its office, by propagating through a series of generations what once had possessed an interest for *them*, but which, under changes of opinion or of taste, had faded to their feelings or had become obsolete for their undertakings, the whole *membrana* or vellum skin, the two-fold product of human skill, costly material, and costly freight of thought, which it carried, drooped in value concurrently—supposing that each were inalienably associated to the other. Once it had been the impress of a human mind which stamped its value upon the vellum; the vellum, though costly, had contributed but a secondary element of value to the total result. At length, however, this relation between the vehicle and its freight has gradually been undermined. The vellum, from having been the setting of the jewel, has risen at length to be the jewel itself; and the burden of thought, from having given the chief value to the vellum, has now become the chief obstacle to its value; nay, has totally extinguished its value, unless it can be dissociated from the connection. Yet, if this unlinking *can* be effected, then, fast as the inscription upon the membrane is sinking into rubbish, the membrane itself is reviving in its separate importance; and, from bearing a ministerial value, the vellum has come at last to absorb the whole value.

Hence the importance for our ancestors that the separation *should* be effected. Hence it arose in the middle ages, as a considerable object for chemistry, to discharge the writing from the roll, and thus to make it available for a new succession of thoughts. The soil, if cleansed from what once had been hot-house plants, but now were held to be weeds, would be ready to receive a fresh and more appropriate crop. In that object the monkish chemist succeeded; but after a fashion which seems almost incredible, incredible not as regards the extent of their success, but as regards the delicacy of restraints under which it moved,—so equally adjusted was their success to the immediate interests of that period, and to the reversionary objects of our own. They did the thing; but not so radically as to prevent us, their posterity, from undoing it. They expelled the writing sufficiently to leave a field for the new manuscript, and yet not sufficiently to make the traces of the elder manuscript irrecoverable for us. Could magic, could Hermes Trismegistus, have done more? What would you think, fair reader, of a problem such as this,—to write a book which should be sense for your own generation, nonsense for the next, should revive into sense for the next after that, but again become nonsense for the fourth; and so on by alternate successions, sinking into night or blazing into day, like the Sicilian river Arethusa, and the English river Mole; or like the undulating motions of a flattened stone which children cause to skim the breast of a river, now diving below the water, now grazing its surface, sinking heavily into darkness, rising buoyantly into light, through a long vista of alternations? Such a problem, you say, is impossible. But really it is a problem not harder apparently than to bid a generation kill, but so that a subsequent generation may call back into life; bury, but so that posterity may command to rise again. Yet *that* was what the rude chemistry of past ages effected when coming into combination with the reaction from the more refined chemistry of our own. Had *they* been better chemists, had *we* been worse, the mixed result, namely, that, dying for *them*, the flower should revive for *us*, could not have been effected. They did the thing proposed to them: they did it effectually, for they founded upon it all that was wanted: and yet ineffectually, since we unravelled their work; effacing all above which they had superscribed; restoring all below which they had effaced.

Here, for instance, is a parchment which contained some Grecian tragedy, the Agamemnon of Æschylus, or the Phoenissae of Euripides. This had possessed a value almost inappreciable in the eyes of accomplished scholars, continually growing rarer through generations. But four centuries are gone by since the destruction of the Western Empire. Christianity, with towering grandeurs of another class, has founded a different empire; and some bigoted, yet perhaps holy monk, has washed away (as he persuades himself) the heathen's tragedy, replacing it with a monastic legend; which legend is disfigured with fables in its incidents, and yet in a higher sense is true, because interwoven with Christian morals, and with the sublimest of Christian revelations. Three, four, five centuries more, find man still devout as ever; but the language has become obsolete, and even for Christian devotion a new era has arisen, throwing it into the channel of crusading zeal or of chivalrous enthusiasm. The *membrana* is wanted now for a knightly romance— for "my Cid," or Coeur de Lion; for Sir Tristrem, or Lybaeus Disconus. In this way, by means of the imperfect chemistry known to the medieval period, the same roll has served as a conservatory for three separate generations of flowers and fruits, all perfectly different, and yet all specially adapted to the wants of the successive possessors. The Greek tragedy, the monkish legend, the knightly romance, each has ruled its own period. One harvest after another has been gathered into the garners of man through ages far apart. And the same hydraulic machinery has distributed, through the same marble fountains, water, milk, or wine, according to the habits and training of the generations that came to quench their thirst.

Such were the achievements of rude monastic chemistry. But the more elaborate chemistry of our own days has reversed all these motions of our simple ancestors, which results in every stage that to *them* would have realized the most fantastic amongst the promises of thaumaturgy. Insolent vaunt of Paracelsus, that he would restore the original rose or violet out of the ashes settling from its combustion—*that* is now rivalled in this modern achievement. The traces of each successive handwriting, regularly effaced, as had been imagined, have, in the inverse order, been regularly called back: the footsteps of the game pursued, wolf or stag, in each several chase, have been unlinked, and hunted back through all their doubles; and, as the chorus of the Athenian stage unwove through the antistrophe every step that had been mystically woven through the strophe, so, by our modern conjurations of science, secrets of ages remote from each other have been exorcised [22] from the accumulated shadows of centuries. Chemistry, a witch as potent as the Erichtho of Lucan, (Pharsalia, lib. vi. or vii.), has extorted by her torments, from the dust and ashes of forgotten centuries, the secrets of a life extinct for the general eye, but still glowing in the embers. Even the fable of the Phoenix, that secular bird, who propagated his solitary existence, and his solitary births, along the line of centuries, through eternal relays of funeral mists, is but a type of what we have done with Palimpsests. We have backed upon each phoenix in the long *regressus*, and forced him to expose his ancestral phoenix, sleeping in the ashes below his own ashes. Our good old forefathers would have been aghast at our sorceries; and, if they speculated on the propriety of burning Dr. Faustus, *us* they would have burned by acclamation. Trial there would have been none; and they could not otherwise have satisfied their horror of the brazen profligacy marking our modern magic, than by ploughing up the houses of all who had been parties to it, and sowing the ground with salt.

[22] Some readers may be apt to suppose, from all English experience, that the word *exorcise* means properly banishment from the shades. Not so. Citation *from* the shades, or sometimes the torturing coercion of mystic adjurations, is more truly the primary sense.

Fancy not, reader, that this tumult of images, illustrative or allusive, moves under any impulse or purpose of mirth. It is but the coruscation of a restless understanding, often made ten times more so by irritation of the nerves, such as you will first learn to comprehend (its *how* and its *why*) some stage or two ahead. The image, the memorial, the record, which for me is derived from a palimpsest, as to one great fact in our human being, and which immediately I will show you, is but too repellent of laughter; or, even if laughter *had* been possible, it would have been such laughter as oftentimes is thrown off from the fields of ocean [23], laughter that hides, or that seems to evade mustering tumult; foam-bells that weave garlands of phosphoric radiance for one moment round the eddies off gleaming abysses; mimicries of earthborn flowers that for the eye raise phantoms of gayety, as oftentimes for the ear they raise the echoes of fugitive laughter, mixing with the ravings and choir-voices of an angry sea.

[23] "Laughter from the fields of ocean."—Many readers will recall, though at the moment of writing my own thoughts did *not* recall, the well-known passage in the Prometheus—

$$—\pi o \nu \tau \omega \nu \ \tau \varepsilon \ \kappa \upsilon \mu \alpha \tau \omega \nu$$
$$\text{‘Aνηριθμον γελασμα.}$$

"Oh multitudinous laughter of the ocean billows!" It is not clear whether Æschylus contemplated the laughter as addressing the ear or the eye.

What else than a natural and mighty palimpsest is the human brain? Such a palimpsest is my brain; such a palimpsest, oh reader! is yours. Everlasting layers of ideas, images, feelings, have fallen upon your brain softly as light. Each succession has seemed to bury all that went before. And yet, in reality, not one has been extinguished. And if, in the vellum palimpsest, lying amongst the other *diplomata* of human archives or libraries, there is anything fantastic or which moves to laughter, as oftentimes there is in the grotesque collisions of those successive themes, having no natural connection, which by pure accident have consecutively occupied the roll, yet, in our own heaven-created palimpsest, the deep memorial palimpsest of the brain, there are not and cannot be such incoherencies. The fleeting accidents of a man's life, and its external shows, may indeed be irrelate and incongruous; but the organizing principles which fuse into harmony, and gather about fixed predetermined centres, whatever heterogeneous elements life may have accumulated from without, will not permit the grandeur of human unity greatly to be violated, or its ultimate repose to be troubled, in the retrospect from dying moments, or from other great convulsions.

Such a convulsion is the struggle of gradual suffocation, as in drowning; and, in the original Opium Confessions , I mentioned a case of that nature communicated to me by a lady from her own childish experience. The lady is still living, though now of unusually great age; and I may mention that amongst her faults never was numbered any levity of principle, or carelessness of the most scrupulous veracity; but, on the contrary, such faults as arise from austerity, too harsh, perhaps, and gloomy, indulgent neither to others nor herself. And, at the time of relating this incident, when already very old, she had become religious to asceticism. According to my present belief, she had completed her ninth year, when, playing by the side of a solitary brook, she fell into one of its deepest pools. Eventually, but after what lapse of time nobody ever knew, she was saved from death by a farmer, who, riding in some distant lane, had seen her rise to the surface; but not until she had descended within the abyss of death, and looked into its secrets, as far, perhaps, as ever human eye can have looked that had permission to return. At a certain stage of this descent, a blow seemed to strike her, phosphoric radiance sprang forth from her eyeballs; and immediately a mighty theatre expanded within her brain. In a moment, in the twinkling of an eye, every act, every design of her past life, lived again, arraying themselves not as a succession, but as parts of a coexistence. Such a light fell upon the whole path of her life backwards into the shades of infancy, as the light, perhaps; which wrapt the destined Apostle on his road to Damascus. Yet that light blinded for a season; but hers poured celestial vision upon the brain, so that her consciousness became omnipresent at one moment to every feature in the infinite review.

This anecdote was treated sceptically at the time by some critics. But, besides that it has since been confirmed by other experience essentially the same, reported by other parties in the same circumstances, who had never heard of each other, the true point for astonishment is not the *simultaneity* of arrangement under which the past events of life, though in fact successive, had formed their dread line of revelation. This was but a secondary phenomenon; the deeper lay in the resurrection itself, and the possibility of resurrection, for what had so long slept in the dust. A pall, deep as oblivion, had been thrown by life over every trace of these experiences; and yet suddenly, at a silent command, at the signal of a blazing rocket sent up from the brain, the pall draws up, and the whole depths of the theatre are exposed. Here was the greater mystery: now this mystery is liable to no doubt; for it is repeated, and ten thousand times repeated, by opium, for those who are its martyrs.

Yes, reader, countless are the mysterious hand-writings of grief or joy which have inscribed themselves successively upon the palimpsest of your brain; and, like the annual leaves of aboriginal forests, or the undissolving snows on the Himalaya, or light falling upon light, the endless strata have covered up each other in forgetfulness. But by the hour of death, but by fever, but by the searchings of opium, all these can revive in strength. They are not dead, but sleeping. In the illustration imagined by myself, from the case of some individual palimpsest, the Grecian tragedy had seemed to be displaced, but was not displaced, by the monkish legend; and the monkish legend had seemed to be displaced, but was not displaced, by the knightly romance. In some potent convulsion of the system, all wheels back into its earliest elementary stage. The bewildering romance, light tarnished with darkness, the semi-fabulous legend, truth celestial mixed with human falsehoods, these fade even of themselves, as life advances. The romance has perished that the young man adored; the legend has gone that deluded the boy; but the deep, deep

48

tragedies of infancy, as when the child's hands were unlinked forever from his mother's neck, or his lips forever from his sister's kisses, these remain lurking below all, and these lurk to the last. Alchemy there is none of passion or disease that can scorch away these immortal impresses; and the dream which closed the preceding section, together with the succeeding dreams of this (which may be viewed as in the nature of choruses winding up the overture contained in Part I.), are but illustrations of this truth, such as every man probably will meet experimentally who passes through similar convulsions of dreaming or delirium from any similar or equal disturbance in his nature [24].

[24] This, it may be said, requires a corresponding duration of experience; but, as an argument for this mysterious power lurking in our nature, I may remind the reader of one phenomenon open to the notice of every body, viz. the tendency of very aged persons to throw back and concentrate the light of their memory upon scenes of early childhood, as to which they recall many traces that had faded even to *themselves* in middle life, while they often forget altogether the whole intermediate stages of their experience. This shows that naturally, and without violent agencies, the human brain is by tendency a palimpsest.

LEVANA AND OUR LADIES OF SORROW

OFTENTIMES at Oxford I saw Levana in my dreams. I knew her by her Roman symbols. Who is Levana? Reader, that do not pretend to have leisure for very much scholarship, you will not be angry with me for telling you. Levana was the Roman goddess that performed for the new-born infant the earliest office of ennobling kindness,—typical, by its mode, of that grandeur which belongs to man everywhere, and of that benignity in powers invisible which even in Pagan worlds sometimes descends to sustain it. At the very moment of birth, just as the infant tasted for the first time the atmosphere of our troubled planet, it was laid on the ground. *That* might bear different interpretations. But immediately, lest so grand a creature should grovel there for more than one instant, either the paternal hand, as proxy for the goddess Levana, or some near kinsman, as proxy for the father, raised it upright, bade it look erect as the king of all this world, and presented its forehead to the stars, saying, perhaps, in his heart, "Behold what is greater than yourselves!" This symbolic act represented the function of Levana. And that mysterious lady, who never revealed her face (except to me in dreams), but always acted by delegation, had her name from the Latin verb (as still it is the Italian verb) *levare*, to raise aloft.

This is the explanation of Levana. And hence it has arisen that some people have understood by Levana the tutelary power that controls the education of the nursery. She, that would not suffer at his birth even a prefigurative or mimic degradation for her awful ward, far less could be supposed to suffer the real degradation attaching to the non-development of his powers. She therefore watches over human education. Now, the word *educo*, with the penultimate short, was derived (by a process often exemplified in the crystallization of languages) from the word *educo*, with the penultimate long. Whatsoever *educes*, or develops, *educates*. By the education of Levana, therefore, is meant,—not the poor machinery that moves by spelling-books and grammars, but by that mighty system of central forces hidden in the deep bosom of human life, which by passion, by strife, by temptation, by the energies of resistance, works forever upon children,—resting not day or night, any more than the mighty wheel of day and night themselves, whose moments, like restless spokes, are glimmering [25] forever as they revolve.

[25] "Glimmering."—As I have never allowed myself to covet any man's ox nor his ass, nor any thing that is his, still less would it become a philosopher to covet other people's images, or metaphors. Here, therefore, I restore to Mr Wordsworth this fine image of the revolving wheel, and the glimmering spokes, as applied by him to the flying successions of day and night. I borrowed it for one moment in order to point my own sentence; which being done, the reader is witness that I now pay it back instantly by a note made for that sole purpose. On the same principle I often borrow their seals from young ladies—when closing my letters. Because there is sure to be some tender sentiment upon them about "memory," or "hope," or "roses," or "reunion:" and my correspondent must be a sad brute who is not touched by the eloquence of the seal, even if his taste is so bad that he remains deaf to mine.

If, then, *these* are the ministries by which Levana works, how profoundly must she reverence the agencies of grief! But you, reader! think,—that children generally are not liable to grief such as mine. There are two senses in the word *generally*, - the sense of Euclid, where it means *universally* (or in the whole extent of the *genus*), and a foolish sense of this world, where it means *usually*. Now, I am far from saying that children universally are capable of grief like mine. But there are more than you ever heard of who die of grief in this island of ours. I will tell you a common case. The rules of Eton require that a boy on the *foundation* should be there twelve years: he is superannuated at eighteen, consequently he must come at six. Children torn away from mothers and sisters at that age not unfrequently die. I speak of what I know. The complaint is not entered by the registrar as grief; but *that* it is. Grief of that sort, and at that age, has killed more than ever have been counted amongst its martyrs.

Therefore it is that Levana often communes with the powers that shake map's heart: therefore it is that she dotes upon grief. "These ladies," said I softly to myself, on seeing the ministers with whom Levana was conversing, " these are the Sorrows; and they are three in number, as the *Graces* are three, who dress man's life with beauty: the *Parcae* are three, who weave the dark arras of man's life in their mysterious loom always with colors sad in part, sometimes angry with tragic crimson and black; the Furies are three, who visit with retributions called from the other side of the grave offences that walk upon this; and at once even the *Muses* were but three, who fit the harp, the trumpet, or the. lute, to the great burdens of man's impassioned creations. These are the Sorrows, all three of whom I know." The last words I say *now*; but in Oxford I said, " one of whom I know, and the others too surely I *shall* know." For already, in my fervent youth, I saw (dimly relieved upon the dark back-ground of my dreams) the imperfect lineaments of the awful sisters. these sisters -by what name shall we call them?

If I say simply, "The Sorrows," there will be a chance of mistaking the term; it might be understood of individual sorrow,—separate cases of sorrow,—whereas I. want a term expressing the mighty abstractions that incarnate themselves in all individual sufferings of man's heart; and I wish to have these abstractions presented as impersonations, that is, as clothed with human attributes of life, and with functions pointing to flesh. Let us call them, therefore, *Our Ladies of Sorrow*. I know them thoroughly, and have walked in all their kingdoms. Three sisters they are, of one mysterious household; and their paths are wide apart; but of their dominion there is no end. Them I saw often conversing with Levana, and sometimes about myself. Do they talk, then? O, no! Mighty phantoms like these disdain the infirmities of language. They may utter voices through the organs of man when they dwell in human hearts, but amongst themselves is no voice nor sound; eternal silence reigns in *their* kingdoms. *They* spoke not as they talked with Levana; they whispered not; they sang not; though oftentimes me thought they *might* have sung: for I upon earth had heard their mysteries oftentimes deciphered by harp and timbrel, by dulcimer and organ. Like God, whose servants they are, they utter their pleasure not by sounds that perish, or by words that go astray, but by signs in heaven, by changes on earth, by pulses in secret rivers, heraldries painted on darkness, and hieroglyphics written on the tablets of the brain. *They* wheeled in mazes; I spelled the steps. *They* telegraphed from afar; *I* read the signals. *They* conspired together; and on the mirrors of darkness *my* eye traced the plots. *Theirs* were the symbols; *mine* are the words.

What is it the sisters are? What is it that they do? Let me describe their form, and their presence; if form it were that still fluctuated in its outline; or presence it were that forever advanced to the front, or forever receded amongst shades.

The eldest of the three is named *Mater Lachrymarum*, Our Lady of Tears. She it is that night and day raves and moans, calling for vanished faces. She stood in Rama, where a voice was heard of lamentation,—Rachel weeping for her children, and refused to be comforted. She it was that stood in Bethlehem on the night when Herod's sword swept its nurseries of Innocents, and the little feet were stiffened forever, which, heard at times as they tottered along floors overhead, woke pulses of love in household hearts that were not unmarked in heaven.

Her eyes are sweet and subtle, wild and sleepy, by turns; oftentimes rising to the clouds, oftentimes challenging the heavens. She wears a diadem round her head. Arid I knew by childish memories that she could go abroad upon the winds, when she heard that sobbing of litanies, or the thundering of organs, and when she beheld the mustering of summer clouds. This sister, the elder, it is that carries keys more than papal at her girdle, which open every cottage and every palace. She, to my knowledge, sate all last summer by the bedside of the blind beggar, him that so often and so gladly I talked with, whose pious daughter, eight years old, with the sunny countenance, resisted the temptations of play and village mirth to travel all day long on dusty roads with her afflicted father. For this did God send her a great reward. In the spring-time of the year, and whilst yet her own spring was budding, he recalled her to himself. But her blind father mourns forever over her; still he dreams at midnight that the little guiding hand is locked within his own; and still he wakens to a darkness that is now within a second and a deeper darkness. This *Mater Lachrymarum* also has been sitting all this winter of 1844-5 within the bedchamber of the Czar, bringing before his eyes a daughter (not less pious) that vanished to God not less suddenly, and left behind her a darkness not less profound. By the power of her keys it is that Our Lady of Tears glides a ghostly intruder into the chambers of sleepless men, sleepless women, sleepless children, from Ganges to the Nile, from Nile to Mississippi. And her, because she is the first-born of her house, and has the widest empire, let us honor with the title of "Madonna."

The second sister is called *Mater Suspiriorum*, Our Lady of Sighs. She never scales the clouds, nor walks abroad upon the winds. She wears no diadem. And her eyes, if they were ever seen, would be neither sweet nor subtle; no man could read their story; they would be found filled with perishing dreams, and with wrecks of forgotten delirium. But she raises not her eyes; her head, on which sits a dilapidated turban, droops forever, forever fastens on the dust. She weeps not. She groans not. But she sighs inaudibly at intervals. Her sister Madonna is oftentimes stormy and frantic, raging in the highest against heaven, and demanding back her darlings. But Our Lady of Sighs never clamors, never defies, dreams not of rebellious aspirations. She is humble to abjectness. Hers is the meekness that belongs to the hopeless. Murmur she may, but it is in her sleep. Whisper she may, but it is to herself in the twilight. Mutter she does at times, but it is in solitary places that are desolate as she is desolate, in ruined cities, and when the sun has gone down to his rest. This sister is the visitor of the Pariah, of the Jew, of the bondsman to the oar in the Mediterranean galleys; of the English criminal in Norfolk Island, blotted out from the books of remembrance in sweet far-off England; of the baffled penitent reverting his eyes forever upon a solitary grave, which to him seems the altar overthrown of some past and bloody sacrifice, on which altar no oblations can now be availing, whether towards pardon that he might implore, or towards reparation that he might attempt. Every slave that at noonday looks up to the tropical sun with timid reproach, as he points with one hand to the earth, our general mother, but for him a step-mother,-as he points with the other hand to the Bible, our general teacher, but against *him* sealed and sequestered [26];—every woman sitting in darkness, without love to shelter her head, or hope to illumine her solitude, because the heaven-born instincts kindling in her nature germs of holy affections, which God implanted in her womanly bosom, having been stifled by social necessities, now burn sullenly to waste, like sepulchral lamps amongst the ancients; every nun defrauded of her unreturning May-time by wicked kinsman, whom God will judge; every captive in every dungeon; all that are betrayed, and all that are rejected; outcasts by traditionary law, and children of *hereditary* disgrace,—all these walk with Our Lady of Sighs. She also carries a key; but she needs it little. For her kingdom is chiefly amongst the tents of Shem, and the houseless vagrant of every clime. Yet in the very highest ranks of man she finds chapels of her own; and even in glorious England there are some that, to the world, carry their heads as proudly as the reindeer, who yet secretly have received her mark upon their foreheads.

[26] This, the reader will be aware, applies chiefly to the cotton and tobacco States of North America; but not to them only: on which account I have not scrupled to figure the sun, which looks down upon slavery, as tropical—no matter if strictly within the tropics, or simply so near to them as to produce a similar climate.

But the third sister, who is also the youngest! Hush! whisper whilst we talk of *her*! Her kingdom is not large, or else no flesh should live; but within that kingdom all power is hers. Her head, turreted like that of Cybèle, rises almost beyond the reach of sight. She droops not; and her eyes rising so high might be hidden by distance. But, being what they are, they cannot be hidden; through the treble veil of crape which she wears, the fierce light of a blazing misery, that rests not for matins or for vespers, for noon of day or noon of night, for ebbing or for flowing tide, may be read from the very ground. She is the defier of God. She also is the mother of lunacies, and the suggestress of suicides. Deep lie the roots of her power; but narrow is the nation that she rules. For she can approach only those in whom a profound nature has been upheaved by central convulsions; in whom the heart trembles and the brain rocks under conspiracies of tempest from without and tempest from within. Madonna moves with uncertain steps, fast or slow, but still with tragic grace. Our Lady of Sighs creeps timidly and stealthily. But. this youngest sister moves with incalculable motions, bounding, and with a tiger's leaps. She carries no key; for, though coming rarely amongst men, she storms all doors at which she is permitted to enter at all. And *her* name is *Mater Tenebrarum*—Our Lady of Darkness.

These were the *Semnai Theai*, or Sublime Goddesses [27],these were the *Eumenides*, or Gracious Ladies (so called by antiquity in shuddering propitiation) of my Oxford dreams. Madonna spoke. She spoke by her mysterious hand. Touching my head, she beckoned to Our Lady of Sighs; and *what* she spoke, translated out of the signs which (except in dreams) no man reads, was this:—

[27] "Sublime Goddesses."—The word σεμνος is usually rendered *venerable* in dictionaries; not a very flattering epithet for females. But by weighing a number of passages in which the word is used pointedly, I am disposed to think that it comes nearest to our idea of the *sublime*; as near as a Greek word *could* come.

"Lo! here is he, whom in childhood I dedicated to my altars. This is he that once I made my darling. Him I led astray, him I beguiled, and from heaven I stole away his young heart to mine. Through me did he become idolatrous; and through me it was, by languishing desires, that he worshipped the worm, and prayed to the wormy grave. Holy was the grave to him; lovely was its darkness; saintly its corruption. Him, this young idolater, I have seasoned for thee, dear gentle Sister of Sighs! Do thou take him now to *thy* heart, and season him for our dreadful sister. And thou,"-turning to the *Mater Tenebrarum*, she said, -"wicked sister, that temptest and hatest, do thou take him from *her*. See that thy sceptre lie heavy on his head. Suffer not woman and her tenderness to sit near him in his darkness. Banish the frailties of hope, wither the relenting of love, scorch the fountains of tears, curse him as only thou canst curse. So shall he be accomplished in the furnace, so shall he see the things that ought *not* to be seen, sights that are abominable, and secrets that are unutterable. So shall he read elder truths, sad truths, grand truths, fearful truths. So shall he rise again *before* he dies. And so shall our commission be accomplished which from God we had, -to plague his heart until we had unfolded the capacities of his spirit [28]."

[28] The reader, who wishes at all to understand the course of these Confessions, ought not to pass over this dream-legend. There is no great wonder that a vision, which occupied my waking thoughts in those years, should re-appear in my dreams. It was in fact a legend recurring in sleep, most of which I had myself silently written or sculptured in my daylight reveries. But its importance to the present Confessions is this—that it rehearses or prefigures their course. This FIRST part belongs to Madonna. The THIRD belongs to the "Mater Suspiriorum," and will be entitled *The Pariah Worlds*. The FOURTH, which terminates the work, belongs to the "Mater Tenebrarum," and will be entitled *The Kingdom of Darkness*. As to the SECOND, it is an interpolation requisite to the effect of the others; and will be explained in its proper place.

THE APPARITION OF THE BROCKEN

ASCEND with me on this dazzling Whitsunday the Brocken of North Germany. The dawn opened in cloudless beauty; it is a dawn of bridal June; but, as the hours advanced, her youngest sister April, that sometimes cares little for racing across both frontiers of May, frets the bridal lady's sunny temper with sallies of wheeling and careering showers, flying and pursuing, opening and closing, hiding and restoring. On such a morning, and reaching the summits of the forest mountain about sunrise, we shall have one chance the more for seeing the famous Spectre of the Brocken [29]. Who and what is he? He is a solitary apparition, in the sense of loving solitude; else he is not always solitary in his personal manifestations, but, on proper occasions, has been known to unmask a strength quite sufficient to alarm those who had been insulting him.

[29] "*Spectre of the Brocken.*"—This very striking phenomenon has been continually described by writers, both German and English, for the last fifty years. Many readers, however, will not have met with these descriptions: and on *their* account I add a few words in explanation; referring them for the best scientific comment on the case to Sir David Brewster's "Natural Magic." The spectre takes the shape of a human figure, or, if the visitors are more than one, then the spectres multiply; they arrange themselves on the blue ground of the sky, or the dark ground of any clouds that may be in the right quarter, or perhaps they are strongly relieved against a curtain of rock, at a distance of some miles, and always exhibiting gigantic proportions. At first, from the distance and the colossal size, every spectator supposes the appearance to be quite independent of himself. But very soon he is surprised to observe his own motions and gestures mimicked; and wakens to the conviction that the phantom is but a dilated reflection of himself. This Titan amongst the apparitions of earth is exceedingly capricious, vanishing abruptly for reasons best known to himself, and more coy in coming forward than the Lady Echo of Ovid. One reason why he is seen so seldom must be ascribed to the concurrence of conditions under which only the phenomenon can be manifested: the sun must be near to the horizon, (which of itself implies a time of day inconvenient to a person starting from a station as distant as Elbingerode;) the spectator must have his back to the sun; and the air must contain some vapour—but *partially* distributed. Coleridge ascended the Brocken on the Whitsunday of 1799, with a party of English students from Goettingen, but failed to see the phantom; afterwards in England (and under the same three conditions) he saw a much rarer phenomenon, which he described in the following eight lines. I give them from a corrected copy: (the apostrophe in the beginning must be understood as addressed to an ideal conception):—

> "And art thou nothing? Such thou art as when
> The woodman winding westward up the glen
> At wintry dawn, when o'er the sheep-track's maze
> The viewless snow-mist weaves a glist'ning haze,
> Sees full before him gliding without tread,
> An image with a glory round its head:
> This shade he worships for its golden hues,
> And *makes* (not knowing) that which he pursues."

Now, in order to test the nature of this mysterious apparition, we will try two or three experiments upon him. What we fear, and with some reason, is, that as he lived so many ages with foul Pagan sorcerers, and witnessed so many centuries of dark idolatries, his heart may have been corrupted; and that even now his faith may be wavering or impure. We will try.

Make the sign of the cross, and observe whether he repeats it (as on Whitsunday [30] he surely ought to do). Look! he *does* repeat it; but the driving showers perplex the images, and *that*, perhaps, it is which gives him the air of one who acts reluctantly or evasively. Now, again, the sun shines more brightly, and the showers have swept off like squadrons of cavalry- to the rear. We will try him again.

[30] *"On Whitsunday."*—It is singular, and perhaps owing to the temperature and weather likely to prevail in that early part of summer, that more appearances of the spectre have been witnessed on Whitsunday than on any other day.

Pluck an anemone, one of these many anemones which once was called the sorcerer's flower [31], and bore a part, perhaps, in this horrid ritual of fear; carry it to that stone which mimics the outline of a heathen altar, and once was called the sorcerer's altar [31];then bending your knee, and raising your right hand to God, say,—" Father, which art in heaven, this lovely anemone, that once glorified the worship of fear, has travelled back into thy fold; this altar, which once reeked with bloody rites to Cortho, has long been rebaptized into thy holy service. The darkness is gone; the cruelty is gone which the darkness bred; the moans have passed away which the victims uttered; the cloud has vanished which once sate continually upon their graves, cloud of protestation that ascended forever to thy throne from the tears of the defenceless, and the anger of the just. And lo! I thy servant, with this dark phantom, whom for one hour on this thy festival of Pentecost I make *my* servant, render thee united worship in this thy recovered temple."

[31] *"The sorcerer's flower,"* and *"the sorcerer's altar."*—These are names still clinging to the anemone of the Brocken, and to an altar-shaped fragment of granite near one of the summits; and it is not doubted that they both connect themselves through links of ancient tradition with the gloomy realities of Paganism, when the whole Hartz and the Brocken formed for a very long time the last asylum to a ferocious but perishing idolatry.

Look now! the apparition plucks an anemone, and places it on an altar; he also bends his knee, he also raises his right hand to God. Dumb he is; but sometimes the dumb serve God acceptably. Yet still it occurs to you, that perhaps on this high festival of the Christian church he may be overruled by supernatural influence into confession of his homage, having so often been made to bow and bend his knee at murderous rites. In a service of religion he may be timid. Let us try him, therefore, with an earthly passion, where he will have no bias either from favor or from fear.

If, then, once in childhood you suffered an affection that was ineffable, -if once, when powerless to face such an enemy, you were summoned to fight with the tiger that couches within the separations of the grave,—in that case, after the example of Judaea (on the Roman coins),—sitting under her palm-tree to weep, but sitting with her head veiled,—do you also veil your head. Many years are passed away since then; and you were a little ignorant thing at that time, hardly above six years old; or perhaps (if you durst tell all the truth), not quite so much. But your heart was deeper than the Danube; and, as was your love, so was your grief. {Many years are gone since that darkness settled on your head; many summers, many winters; yet still its shadows wheel round upon you at intervals, like these April showers upon this glory of bridal June. Therefore now, on this dovelike morning of Pentecost, do you veil your head like Judaea in memory of that transcendent woe, and in testimony that, indeed, it surpassed all utterance of words. Immediately you see that the apparition of the Brocken veils his head, after the model of Judaea weeping under her palm-tree, as if he also had a human heart, and that *he* also, in childhood, having suffered an affliction which was ineffable, wished by these mute symbols to breathe a sigh towards heaven in memory of that affliction, and by way of record, though many a year after, that it was indeed unutterable by words.

This trial is decisive. You are now satisfied that the apparition is but a reflex of yourself; and, in uttering your secret feelings to *him*, you make this phantom the dark symbolic mirror for reflection to the daylight what else must be hidden for ever.

Such a relation does the Dark Interpreter, whom immediately the reader will learn to know as an intruder into my dreams, bear to my own mind. He is originally a mere reflex of my inner nature. But as the apparition of the Brocken sometimes is disturbed by storms or by driving showers, so as to dissemble his real origin, in like manner the Interpreter sometimes swerves out of my orbit, and mixes a little with alien natures. I do not always know him in these cases as my own parhelion. What he says, generally, is but that which I have said in daylight, and in meditation deep enough to sculpture itself on my heart. But sometimes, as his face alters, his words alter; and they do not always seem such as I have used, or *could* use. No man can account for all things that occur in dreams. Generally I believe this, —that he is a faithful representative of myself; but he also is at times subject to the action of the good *Phantasus*, who rules in dreams.

Hailstone choruses [32] besides, and storms, enter my dreams. Hailstones and fire that run along the ground, sleet and blinding hurricanes, revelations of glory insufferable pursued by volleying darkness,—these are powers able to disturb any features that originally were but shadow, and so send drifting the anchors of any vessel that rides upon deeps so treacherous as those of dreams. Understand, however, the Interpreter to bear generally the office of a tragic chorus at Athens. The Greek chorus is perhaps not quite understood by critics, any more than the Dark Interpreter by myself. But the leading function of both must be supposed this- not to tell you anything absolutely new,- that was done by the actors in the drama; but to recall you to your own lurking thoughts,—hidden for the moment or imperfectly developed,—and to place before you, in immediate connection with groups vanishing too quickly for any effort of meditation on your own part, such commentaries, prophetic or looking back, pointing the moral or deciphering the mystery, justifying Providence, or mitigating the fierceness of anguish, as would or might have occurred to your own meditative heart, had only time been allowed for its motions.

[32] *"Hailstone choruses."*—I need not tell any lover of Handel that his oratorio of "Israel in Egypt" contains a chorus familiarly known by this name. The words are—"And he gave them hailstones for rain; fire, mingled with the hail, ran along upon the ground."

The Interpreter is anchored and stationary in my dreams; but great storms and driving mists cause him to fluctuate uncertainly, or even to retire altogether, like his gloomy counterpart, the shy phantom of the Brocken,- and to assume new features or strange features, as in dreams always there is a power not contented with reproduction, but which absolutely creates or transforms. This dark being the reader will see again in a further stage of my opium experience; and I warn him that he will not always be found sitting inside my dreams, but at times outside, and in open daylight.

FINALE TO PART I—SAVANNAH-LA-MAR

God smote Savannah-la-mar, and in one night, by earthquake, removed her, with all her towers standing and population sleeping, from the steadfast foundations of the shore to the coral floors of ocean. And God said,—Pompeii did I bury and conceal from men through seventeen centuries: this city I will bury, but not conceal. She shall be a monument to men of my mysterious anger, set in azure light through generations to come; for I will enshrine her in a crystal dome of my tropic seas." This city, therefore, like a mighty galleon with all her apparel mounted, streamers flying, and tackling perfect, seems floating along the noiseless depths of ocean; and oftentimes in glassy calms, through the translucid atmosphere of water that now stretches like an air-woven awning above the silent encampment, mariners from every clime look down into her courts and terraces, count her gates, and number the spires of her churches. She is one ample cemetery, and has been for many a year; but in the mighty calms that brood for weeks over tropic latitudes, she fascinates the eye with a *Fata-Morgana* revelation, as of human life still subsisting in submarine asylums sacred from the storms that torment our upper air.

Thither, lured by the loveliness of cerulean depths, by the peace of human dwellings privileged from molestation, by the gleam of marble altars sleeping in everlasting sanctity, oftentimes in dreams did I and the Dark Interpreter cleave the watery veil that divided us from her streets. We looked into the belfries, where the pendulous bells were waiting in vain for the summons which should awaken their marriage peals; together we touched the mighty organ-keys, that sang no *jubilates* for the ear of Heaven, that sang no requiems for the ear of human sorrow; together we searched the silent nurseries, where the children were all asleep, and *had* been asleep through five generations. "They are waiting for the heavenly dawn," whispered the Interpreter to himself: " and, when *that* comes, the bells and the organs will utter a *jubilate* repeated by the echoes of Paradise." Then, turning to me, he said,—"This is sad, this is piteous; but less would not have sufficed for the purpose of God. Look here. Put into a Roman clepsydra one hundred drops of water; let these run out as the sands in an hour-glass; every drop measuring the hundredth part of a second, so that each shall represent but the three-hundred-and-sixty-thousandth part of an hour. Now, count the drops as they race along; and, when the fiftieth of the hundred is passing, behold! forty-nine are -not, because already they have perished; and fifty are not, because they are yet to come. You see, therefore, how narrow, how incalculably narrow, is the true and actual present. Of that time which we call the present, hardly a hundredth part but belongs either to a past which has fled, or to a future which is still on the wing. It has perished, or it is not born. It was, or it is not. Yet even this approximation to the truth is *infinitely* false. For again subdivide that solitary drop, which only was found to represent the present, into a lower series of similar fractions, and the actual present which you arrest measures now but the thirty-sixth-millionth of an hour; and so by infinite declensions the true and very present, in which only we live and enjoy, will vanish into a mote of a mote, distinguishable only by a heavenly vision. Therefore the present, which only man possesses, offers less capacity for his footing than the slenderest film that ever spider twisted from her womb. Therefore, also, even this incalculable shadow from the narrowest pencil of moonlight is more transitory than geometry can measure, or thought of angel can overtake. The time which *is* contracts into a mathematic point; and even that point perishes a thousand times before we can utter its birth. All is finite in the present; and even that finite is infinite in its velocity of flight towards death. But in God there is nothing finite; but in God there is nothing transitory; but in God there *can* be nothing that tends to death. Therefore, it follows, that for God there can be no present. The future is the present of God, and to the future it is that he sacrifices the human present. Therefore it is that he works by earthquake. Therefore it is that he works by grief. O, deep is the ploughing of earthquake! O, deep "- [and his voice swelled like a *sanctus* rising from the choir of a cathedral]—"O, deep is the ploughing of grief! But oftentimes less would not suffice for the agriculture of God. Upon a night of earthquake he builds a thousand years of pleasant habitations for man. Upon the sorrow of an infant he raises oftentimes from human intellects glorious vintages that could not else have been. Less than these fierce ploughshares would not have stirred the stubborn soil. The one is needed for earth, our planet, -for earth itself as the dwelling-place of man; but the other is needed yet oftener for God's mightiest instrument,—yes " [and he looked solemnly at myself], "is needed for the mysterious children of the earth!"

END OF PART I

PART II

The Oxford visions, of which some have been given, were but anticipations necessary to illustrate the glimpse opened of childhood (as being its reaction). In this SECOND part, returning from that anticipation, I retrace an abstract of my boyish and youthful days, so far as they furnished or exposed the germs of later experiences in worlds more shadowy.

Upon me, as upon others scattered thinly by tens and twenties over every thousand years, fell too powerfully and too early the vision of life. The horror of life mixed itself already in earliest youth with the heavenly sweetness of life; that grief, which one in a hundred has sensibility enough to gather from the sad retrospect of life in its closing stage, for me shed its dews as a prelibation upon' the fountains of life whilst yet sparkling to the morning sun. I saw from afar and from before what I was to see from behind. Is this the description of an early youth passed in the shades of gloom? No; but of a youth passed in the divinest happiness. And if the reader has (which so few have) the passion, without which there is no reading of the legend and superscription upon man's brow, if he is not (as most are) deafer than the grave to every *deep* note that sighs upwards from the Delphic caves of human life, he will know that the rapture of life (or anything which by approach can merit that name) does not arise, unless as perfect music arises, music of Mozart or Beethoven, by the confluence of the mighty and terrific discords with the subtle concords. Not by contrast, or as reciprocal foils, do these elements act, which is the feeble conception of many, but by union. They are the sexual forces in music: "male and female created he them;" and these mighty antagonists do not put forth their hostilities by repulsion, but by deepest attraction.

As "in to-day already walks to-morrow," so in the past experience of a youthful life may be seen dimly the future. The collisions with alien interests or hostile views, of a child, boy, or very young man, so insulated as each of these is sure to be,—those aspects of opposition which such a person *can* occupy,—are limited by the exceedingly few and trivial lines of connection along which he is able to radiate any essential influence whatever upon the fortunes or happiness of others. Circumstances may magnify his importance for the moment; but, after all, any cable which he carries out upon other vessels is easily slipped upon a feud arising. Far otherwise is the state of relations

58

connecting an adult or responsible man with the circles around him, as life advances. The net-work of these relations is a thousand times more intricate, the jarring of these intricate relations a thousand times more frequent, and the vibrations a thousand times harsher which these jarrings diffuse. This truth is felt beforehand misgivingly and in troubled vision, by a young man who stands upon the threshold of manhood. One earliest instinct of fear and horror would darken his spirit, if it could be revealed to itself and self-questioned at the moment of birth: a second instinct of the same nature would again pollute that tremulous mirror, if the moment were as punctually marked as physical birth is marked, which dismisses him finally upon the tides of absolute self-control. A dark ocean would seem the total expanse of life from the first; but far darker and more appalling would seem that interior and second chamber of the ocean which called him away forever from the direct accountability of others. Dreadful would be the morning which should say, "Be thou a human child incarnate;" but more dreadful the morning which should say, "! Bear thou henceforth the sceptre of thy self-dominion through life, and the passion of life!" Yes, dreadful would be both; but without a basis of the dreadful there is no perfect rapture. It is a part through the sorrow of life, growing out of dark events, that this basis of awe and solemn darkness slowly accumulates. *That* I have illustrated. But, as life expands, it is more through the *strife* which besets us, strife from conflicting opinions, positions, passions, interests, that the funereal ground settles and deposits itself, which sends upward the dark lustrous brilliancy through the jewel of life, else revealing a pale and superficial glitter. Either the human being must suffer and struggle as the price of a more searching vision, or his gaze must be shallow, and without intellectual revelation.

Through accident it was in part, and, where through no accident but my own nature, not through features of it at all painful to recollect, that constantly in early life (that is, from boyish days until eighteen, when, by going to Oxford, practically I became my own master) I was engaged in duels of fierce continual struggle, with some person or body of persons, that sought, like the Roman *retiarius*, to throw a net of deadly coercion or constraint over the undoubted rights of my natural freedom. The steady rebellion upon my part in one half was a mere human reaction of justifiable indignation; but in the other half it was the struggle of a conscientious nature, disdaining to feel it as any mere right or discretional privilege,—no, feeling it as the noblest of duties to resist, though it should be mortally, those that would have enslaved me, and to retort scorn upon those that would have put my head below their feet. Too much, even in later life, I have perceived, in men that pass for good men, a disposition to degrade (and if possible to degrade through self-degradation) those in whom unwillingly they feel any weight of oppression to themselves, by commanding qualities of intellect or character. They respect you: they are compelled to do so, and they hate to do so. Next, therefore, they seek tb throw off the sense of this oppression, and to take vengeance for it, by cooperating with any unhappy accidents in your life, to inflict a sense of humiliation upon you, and (if possible) to force you into becoming a consenting party to that humiliation. O, wherefore is it that those who presume to call themselves the "friends" of this man or that woman are so often those, above all others, whom -in the hour of death that man or woman is most likely to salute with the valediction —Would God I had never seen your face?

In citing one or two cases of these early struggles, I have chiefly in view the effect of these upon my subsequent visions under the reign of opium. And this indulgent reflection should accompany the mature reader through all such records of boyish inexperience. A good-tempered man, who is also acquainted with the world, will easily evade, without needing any artifice of servile obsequiousness, those quarrels which an upright simplicity, jealous of its own rights, and unpractised in the science of worldly address, cannot always evade without some loss of self-respect. Suavity in this manner may, it is true, be reconciled with firmness in the matter; but not easily by a young person who wants all the appropriate resources of knowledge, of adroit and guarded language, for making his good temper available. Men are protected from insult and wrong, not merely by their own skill, but also, in the absence of any skill at all, by the general spirit of forbearance to which society has trained all those whom they are likely to meet. But boys meeting with no such forbearance or training in other boys, must sometimes be thrown upon feuds in the ratio of their own firmness, much more than in the ratio of any natural proneness to quarrel. Such a subject, however, will be best illustrated by a sketch or two of my own principal feuds.

The first, but merely transient and playful, nor worth noticing at all, but for its subsequent resurrection under other and awful coloring in my dreams, grew out of an imaginary slight, as I viewed it, put upon me by one of my guardians. I had four guardians; and the one of these who had the most knowledge and talent of the whole - a banker, living about a hundred miles from my home—had invited me, when eleven years old, to his house. His eldest daughter, perhaps a year younger than myself, wore at that time upon her very lovely face the most angelic expression of character and temper that I have almost ever seen. Naturally, I fell in love with her. It seems absurd to say so; and the more so, because two children more absolutely innocent than we were cannot be imagined, neither of us having ever been at any school; but the simple truth is, that in the most chivalrous sense I was in love with her. And the proof that I was so showed itself in three separate modes: I kissed her glove on any rare occasion when I found it lying on a table; secondly, I looked out for some excuse to be jealous of her; and, thirdly, I did my very best to get up a quarrel. What I wanted the quarrel for was the luxury of a reconciliation; a hill cannot be had, you know, without going to the expense of a valley. And though I hated the very thought of a moment's difference with so truly gentle a girl, yet how, but through such a purgatory, could one win the paradise of her returning smiles? All this, however, came to nothing; and simply because she positively would *not* quarrel. And the jealousy fell through, because there was no decent subject for such a passion, unless it had settled upon an old music-master, whom lunacy itself could not adopt as a rival. The quarrel, meantime, which never prospered with the daughter, silently kindled on my part towards the father. His offence was this. At dinner, I naturally placed myself by the side of M., and it gave me great pleasure to touch her hand at intervals. As M. was my cousin, though twice or even three times removed, I did not feel it taking too great a liberty in this little act of tenderness. No matter if three thousand times removed, I said, my cousin is my cousin; nor had I very much designed to conceal the act; or if so, rather on her account than my own. One evening, however, papa observed my maneuver. Did he seem displeased? Not at all; he even condescended to smile. But the next day he placed M. on the side opposite to myself. In one respect this was really an improvement, because it gave me a better view of my cousin's sweet countenance. But then there was the loss of the hand to be' considered, and secondly there was the affront. It was clear that vengeance must be had. Now, there was but one thing in this world that I could do even decently; but *that* I could do admirably. This was writing Latin hexameters. Juvenal— though it was not very much of him that I had then read—seemed to me a divine model. The inspiration of wrath spoke through him as through a Hebrew prophet. The same inspiration spoke now in me. *Facit indignatio versum*, said Juvenal. And it must be owned that indignation has never made such good verses since as she did in that day. But still, even to me, this agile passion proved a Muse of genial inspiration for a couple of paragraphs; and one line I will mention as worthy to have taken its place in Juvenal himself. I say this without scruple, having not a shadow of vanity, nor, on the other hand, a shadow of false modesty connected with such boyish accomplishments. The poem opened thus:—

"Te nimis austerum sacrae qui foedera mensae
Diruis, insector Satyrae reboante flagello."

But the line which I insist upon as of Roman strength was the closing one of the next sentence. The general effect of the sentiment was, that my clamorous wrath should make its way even into ears that were past hearing:

"—mea saeva querela
Auribus insidet ceratis, auribus etsi
Non audituris hybernâ nocte procellam."

The power, however, which inflated my verse, soon collapsed; having been soothed, from the very first, by finding, that except in this one instance at the dinner table, which probably had been viewed as an indecorum, no further restraint, of any kind whatever, was meditated upon my intercourse with M. Besides, it was too painful to lock up good verses in one's own solitary breast. Yet how could I shock the sweet filial heart of my cousin by a fierce lampoon or *stylites* against her father, had Latin even figured amongst her accomplishments? Then it occurred to me that the verses might be shown to the father. But was there not something treacherous in gaining a man's approbation under a mask to a satire upon himself? Or would he have always understood me? For one person, a year after, took the *sacrae mensae* (by which I had meant the sanctities of hospitality) to mean the sacramental table. And on consideration, I began to suspect that many people would pronounce myself the party who had violated the holy ties of hospitality, which are equally binding on guest as on host. Indolence, which sometimes comes in aid of good impulses as well as bad, favored these relenting thoughts. The society of M. did still more to wean me from further efforts of satire; and, finally, my Latin poem remained a torso. But, upon the whole, my guardian had a narrow escape of descending to posterity in a disadvantageous light, had he rolled down to it through my hexameters.

Here was a case of merely playful feud. But the same talent of Latin verses soon after connected me with a real feud, that harassed my mind more than would be supposed, and precisely by this agency, namely, that it arrayed one set of feelings against another. It divided my mind, as by domestic feud, against itself. About a year after returning from the visit to my guardian's, and when I must have been nearly completing my twelfth year, I was sent to a great public school. Every man has reason to rejoice who enjoys so great an advantage. I condemned, and do condemn, the practice of sometimes sending out into such stormy exposures those who are as yet too young, too dependent on female gentleness, and endowed with sensibilities too exquisite. But at nine or ten the masculine energies of the Character are beginning to be developed; or if not, no discipline will better aid in their development than the bracing intercourse of a great English classical school. Even the selfish are forced into accommodating themselves to a public standard of generosity, and the effeminate into conforming to a rule of manliness. I was myself at two public schools; and I think with gratitude of the benefit which I reaped from both; as also I think with gratitude of the upright guardian in whose quiet household I learned Latin so effectually. But the small private schools which I witnessed for brief periods, containing thirty to, forty boys; were models of ignoble manners as respected some part of the juniors, and of favoritism amongst the masters. Nowhere is the sublimity of public justice so broadly exemplified as in an English school. There is not in the universe such an areopagus for fair play, and abhorrence of all crooked ways, as an English mob, or one of the English time-honored public schools. But my own first introduction to such an establishment was under peculiar and contradictory circumstances. When my "rating," or graduation in the school, was to be settled, naturally my altitude (to speak astronomically) was taken by the proficiency in Greek. But I could then barely construe books so easy as the Greek Testament and the Iliad. This was considered quite well enough for my age; but still it caused me to be placed three steps below the highest rank in the school. Within one week, however, my talent for Latin verses, which had by this time gathered strength and expansion, became known. I was honored as never was man or boy since Mordecai the Jew. Not properly belonging to the flock of the head master, but to the leading section of the second, I was now weekly paraded for distinction at the supreme tribunal of the school; out of which at first grew nothing but a sunshine of approbation delightful to my heart, still brooding upon solitude. Within six weeks this had changed. The approbation, indeed, continued, and the public testimony of it. Neither would there, in the ordinary course, have been any painful reaction from jealousy, or fretful resistance to the soundness of my pretensions; since it was sufficiently known to some of my school-fellows, that I, who had no male relatives but military men, and those in India, could not have benefited by any clandestine aid. But, unhappily, the head master was at that time dissatisfied with some points in the progress of his head form; and, as it soon appeared, was continually throwing in their teeth the brilliancy of my verses at twelve, by comparison with theirs at seventeen, eighteen, and nineteen. I had observed him sometimes pointing to myself; and was perplexed at seeing this gesture followed by gloomy looks, and what French reporters call "sensation," in these young men, whom naturally I viewed with awe as my leaders, boys that were called young men, men that were reading Sophocles—(a name that carried with it the sound of something seraphic to my ears), -and who never had vouchsafed to waste a word on such a child as myself. The day was come, however, when all that would be changed. One of these leaders strode up to me in the public play-grounds, and delivering a blow on my shoulder, which was not intended to hurt me, but as a mere formula of introduction, asked me "What the d—l I meant by bolting out of the course, and annoying other people in that manner? Were other people to have no rest for me and my verses, which, after all, were horribly bad?" There might have been some difficulty in returning an answer to this address, but none was required. I was briefly admonished to see that I wrote worse for the future, or else—At this *aposiopesis*, I looked inquiringly at the speaker, and he filled up the chasm by saying that he would "annihilate" me. Could any person fail to be aghast at such a demand? I was to write worse than my own standard, which, by his account of my verses, must be difficult; and I was to write worse than himself, which might be impossible. My feelings revolted, it may be supposed, against so arrogant a demand, unless it had been far otherwise expressed; and on the next occasion for sending up verses, so far from attending to the orders issued, I double-shotted my guns; double applause descended on myself; but I remarked, with some awe, though not repenting of what I had done, that double confusion seemed to agitate the ranks of my enemies. Amongst them loomed out in the distance my "annihilating" friend, who shook his huge fist at me, but with something like a grim smile about his eyes. He took an early opportunity of paying his respects to me, saying, "You little devil, do you call this writing your worst?" "No," I replied; "I call it writing my best." The annihilator, as it turned out, was really a good-natured young man; but he soon went off to Cambridge; and with the rest, or some of them, I continued to wage war for nearly a year. And yet, for a word spoken with kindness, I would have resigned the peacock's feather in my cap as the merest of baubles. Undoubtedly praise sounded sweet in my ears also. But that was nothing by comparison with what stood on the other side. I detested distinctions that were connected with mortification to others. And, even if I could have got over *that*, the eternal feud fretted and tormented my nature. Love, that once in childhood had been so mere a necessity to me, *that* had long been a mere reflected ray from a departed sunset. But peace, and freedom from strife, if love were no longer possible (as so rarely it is in this world), was the absolute necessity of my heart. To contend with somebody was still my fate; how to escape the contention I could not see; and yet for itself, and the deadly passions into which it forced me, I hated and loathed it more than death. It added to the distraction and internal feud of my own mind, that I could not *altogether* condemn the upper boys. I was made a handle of humiliation to them. And, in the mean time, if I had an advantage in one accomplishment, which is all a matter of accident, or peculiar taste and feeling, they, on the other hand, had a great advantage over me in the more elaborate difficulties of Greek, and of choral Greek poetry. I could not altogether wonder at their hatred of myself. Yet still, as they had chosen to adopt this mode of conflict with me, I did not feel that I had any choice but to resist. The contest was terminated for me by my removal from the school, in consequence of a very threatening illness affecting my head; but it lasted nearly a year, and it did not close before several amongst my public enemies had become my private friends. They were much older, but they invited me to the houses of their friends, and showed me a respect which deeply affected me,- this respect having more reference, apparently, to the firmness I had exhibited, than to the splendor of my verses. And, indeed, these had rather drooped, from a natural accident; several persons of my own class had formed the practice of asking me to write verses for *them*. I could not refuse. But, as the subjects given out were the same for all of us, it was not possible to take so many crops off the ground without starving the quality of all.

Two years and a half from this time, I was again at a public school of ancient foundation. Now I was myself one of the three who formed the highest class. Now I myself was familiar with Sophocles, who once had been so shadowy a name in my ear. But, strange to say, now, in my sixteenth year, I cared nothing at all for the glory of Latin verse. All the business of school was light and trivial in my eyes. Costing me not an effort, it could not engage any part of my attention; that was now swallowed up altogether by the literature of my native land. I still reverenced the Grecian drama, as always I must. But else I cared little then for classical pursuits. A deeper spell had mastered me; and I lived only in those bowers where deeper passions spoke.

Here, however, it was that began another and more important struggle. I was drawing near to seventeen, and, in a year after *that*, would arrive the usual time for going to Oxford. To Oxford my guardians made no objection; and they readily agreed to make the allowance then universally regarded as the *minimum* for an Oxford student, namely, £200 per annum. But they insisted, as a previous condition, that I should make a positive and definite choice of a profession. Now, I was well aware, that, if I *did* make such a choice, no law existed, nor could any obligation be created through deeds or signature, by which

I could finally be compelled into keeping my engagement. But this evasion did not suit me. Here, again, I felt indignantly that the principle of the attempt was unjust. The object was certainly to do me service by saving money, since, if I selected the bar as my profession, it was contended by some persons (misinformed, however), that not Oxford, but a special pleader's office, would be my proper destination; but I cared not for arguments of that sort. Oxford I was determined to make my home; and also to bear my future course utterly untrammelled by promises that I might repent. Soon came the catastrophe of this struggle. A little before my seventeenth birth-day, I walked off, one lovely summer morning, to North Wales, rambled there for months, and, finally, under some obscure hopes of raising money on my personal security, I went up to London. Now I was in my eighteenth year, and during this period it was that I passed through that trial of severe distress, of which I gave some account in my former Confessions. Having a motive, however, for glancing backwards briefly at that period in the present series, I will do so at this point.

I saw in one journal an insinuation that the incidents in the *preliminary* narrative were possibly without foundation. To such an expression of mere gratuitous malignity, as it happened to be supported by no one argument, except a remark, apparently absurd, but certainly false, I did not condescend to answer. In reality, the possibility had never occurred to me that any person of judgment would seriously suspect me of taking liberties with that part of the work, since, though no one of the parties concerned but myself stood in so central a position to the circumstances as to be acquainted with *all* of them, many were acquainted with each separate section of the memoir. Relays of witnesses might have been summoned to mount guard, as it were, upon the accuracy of each particular in the whole succession of incidents; and some of these people had an interest, more or less strong, in exposing any deviation from the strictest *letter* of the truth, had it been in their power to do so. It is now twenty-two years since I saw the objection here alluded to; and in saying that I did not condescend to notice it, the reader must not find any reason for taxing me with a blamable haughtiness. But every man is entitled to be haughty when his veracity is impeached; and still more when it is impeached by a dishonest objection, or, if not *that*, by an objection which argues a carelessness of attention almost amounting to dishonesty, in a case where it was meant to sustain an imputation of falsehood. Let a man read carelessly, if he will, but not where he is meaning to use his reading for a purpose of wounding another man's honor. Having thus, by twenty-two years' silence, sufficiently expressed my contempt for the slander [33], I now feel myself at liberty to draw it into notice, for the sake, *inter alia*, of showing in how rash a spirit malignity often works. In the preliminary account of certain boyish adventures which had exposed me to suffering of a kind not commonly incident to persons in my station in life, and leaving behind a temptation to the. use of opium under certain arrears of weakness, I had occasion to notice a disreputable attorney in London, who showed me some attentions, partly on my own account as a boy of some expectations, but much more with the purpose of fastening his professional grappling-hooks upon the young Earl of A—t, my former companion, and my present correspondent. This man's house was slightly described, and, with more minuteness, I had exposed some interesting traits in his household economy. A question, therefore, naturally arose in several people's curiosity—Where was this house situated? and the more so because I had pointed a renewed attention to it by saying, that on that very evening (namely, the evening on which that particular page of the Confessions was written) I had visited the street, looked up at the windows, and, instead of the gloomy desolation reigning there when. myself and a little girl were the sole nightly tenants, sleeping, in fact (poor freezing creatures that we both, were), on the floor of the attorney's law-chamber, ands making a pillow out of his infernal parchments,—I had seen, with pleasure, the evidences of comfort, respectability, and domestic animation, in the lights and stir prevailing through different stories of the house. Upon this, the upright critic told his readers that I had described the house as standing in Oxford-street, and then appealed to their own knowledge of that street whether such a house could be so situated. Why not—he neglected to tell us. The houses at the east end of Oxford-street are certainly of too small an order to meet my account of the attorney's house; but why should it be at the east end? Oxford-street is a mile and a quarter long, and, being built continuously on both sides, finds room for houses of many classes. Meantime it happens that, although the true house was most obscurely indicated, *any* house whatever in Oxford-street was most luminously excluded. In all the immensity of London there was but one single street that could be challenged by an attentive reader of the Confessions as peremptorily not the street of the attorney's house—and *that* one was Oxford-street; for, in speaking of my own renewed acquaintance with the outside of this house, I used some expression implying that, in order to make such a visit of reconnaissance, I had turned *aside* from Oxford-street. The matter is a perfect trifle in itself, but it is no trifle in a question affecting a writer's accuracy. If in a thing so absolutely impossible to be forgotten as the true situation of a house painfully memorable to a man's feelings, from being the scene of boyish distresses the most exquisite, nights passed in the misery of cold,—and hunger preying upon him, both night and day, in a degree which very many would not have survived, he, when retracing his school-boy annals, could have shown indecision, even far more dreaded inaccuracy, in identifying the house,—not one syllable after *that*, which he could have said on any other subject, would have won any confidence, or deserved any, from a judicious reader. I may now mention—the Herod being dead, whose persecutions I had reason to fear - that the house in question stands in Greek street on the west, and is the house on that side nearest to Soho-square, but without looking into the square. This it was hardly safe to mention at the date of the published Confessions. It was my private opinion, indeed, that there were probably twenty-five chances to one in favor of my friend the attorney having been by that time hanged. But then this argued inversely; one chance to twenty-five that my friend might be *un*hanged, and knocking about the streets of London; in which case it would have been a perfect god-send to him that here lay an opening (of *my* contrivance, not *his*) for requesting the opinion of a jury on the amount of *solatium* due to his wounded feelings in an action on the passage in the Confessions. To have indicated even the street would have been enough; because there could surely be but one such Grecian in Greek-street, or but one that realized the other conditions of the unknown quantity. There was also a separate danger not absolutely so laughable as it sounds. Me there was little chance that the attorney should meet; but my book he might easily have met (supposing always that the warrant of *Sus. per coll.* had not yet on *his* account travelled down to Newgate). For he was literary; admired literature; and, as a lawyer, he wrote on some subjects fluently; might he not publish *his* Confessions? Or, which would be worse, a supplement to mine, printed so as exactly to match? In which case I should have had the same affliction that Gibbon the historian dreaded so much, namely, that of seeing a refutation of himself, and his own answer to the refutation, all bound up in one and the same: self-combating volume. Besides, he would have cross-examined me before the public, in Old Bailey style; no story, the most straightforward that ever was told, could be sure to stand *that*. And my readers might be left in a state of painful doubt, whether *he* might not, after all, have been a model of suffering innocence (to say the kindest thing possible) plagued with the natural treacheries of a schoolboy's memory. In taking leave of this case and the remembrances connected with it, let me say that, although really believing in the probability of the attorney's having at least found his way to Australia, I had no satisfaction in thinking of that result. I knew my friend to be the very perfection of a scamp. And in the running account between us (I mean, in the ordinary sense, as to money), the balance could not be in *his* favor; since I, on receiving a sum of money (considerable in the eyes of us both), had transferred pretty nearly the whole of it to *him*, for the purpose ostensibly held out to me (but of course a hoax) of purchasing certain law "stamps;" for he was then pursuing a diplomatic correspondence with various Jews who lent money to young heirs, in some trifling proportion on my own insignificant account, but much more truly on the account of Lord A—t, my young friend. On the other side, he had given to me simply the relics of his breakfast-table, which itself was hardly more than a relic. But in this he was not to blame. He could not give to me what he had not for himself, nor sometimes for the poor starving child whom I now suppose to have been his illegitimate daughter. So desperate was the running fight, yardarm to yard-arm, which he maintained with creditors fierce as famine and hungry as the grave,—so deep also was his horror (I know not for which of the various reasons supposable) against falling into a prison,—that he seldom ventured to sleep twice successively in the same house. That expense of itself must have pressed heavily in London, where you pay half a crown at least for a bed that would cost only a shilling in the provinces. In the midst of his knaveries, and, what were even more shocking to my remembrance, his confidential discoveries in his rambling conversations of knavish *designs* (not always pecuniary), there was a light of wandering misery in his eye, at times, which affected me afterwards at intervals, when I recalled it in the radiant happiness of nineteen, and amidst the solemn tranquillities of Oxford. That of itself was interesting; the man was worse by far than he had been meant to be; he had not the mind that reconciles itself to evil. Besides, he respected scholarship, which appeared by the deference he generally showed to myself, then about seventeen; he had an interest in literature,—*that* argues something good; and was pleased at any time, or even cheerful, when I turned the conversation upon books; nay, he seemed touched with emotion when I quoted some sentiment noble and impassioned from one of the great poets, and would ask me to repeat it. He would have been a man of memorable energy, and for good purposes, had it not been for his agony of conflict with pecuniary embarrassments. These probably had commenced in some fatal compliance with temptation arising out of funds confided to him by a client. Perhaps he had gained fifty guineas for a moment of necessity, and had sacrificed for that trifle *only* the serenity and the comfort of a life. Feelings of relenting kindness it was not in my nature to refuse in such a case; and I wished to * * * *

[33] Being constantly almost an absentee from London, and very often from other great cities, so as to command oftentimes no favourable opportunities for overlooking the great mass of public journals, it is possible enough that other slanders of the same tenor may have existed. I speak of what met my own eye, or was accidentally reported to me—but in fact all of us are exposed to this evil of calumnies lurking unseen—for no degree of energy, and no excess of disposable tie, would enable any one man to exercise this sort of vigilant police over *all* journals. Better, therefore, tranquilly to leave all such malice to confound itself.

But I never succeeded in tracing his steps through the wilderness of London until some years back, when I ascertained that he was dead. Generally speaking, the few people whom I have disliked in this world were flourishing people, of good repute. Whereas the knaves whom I have known, one and all, and by no means few, I think of with pleasure and kindness.

Heavens! when I look back to the sufferings which I have witnessed or heard of, even from this one brief London experience, I say, if life could throw open its long suites of chambers to our eyes from some station *beforehand*, if, from some secret stand, we could look by *anticipation* along its vast corridors, and aside into the recesses opening upon them from either hand,—halls of tragedy or chambers of retribution, simply in that small wing and no more of the great caravanserai which we ourselves shall haunt,—simply in that narrow tract of time, and no more, where we ourselves shall range, and confining our gaze to those, and no others, for whom personally we shall be interested,—what a recoil we should suffer of horror in our estimate of life! What if those sudden catastrophes, or those inexpiable afflictions, which *have* already descended upon the people within my own knowledge, and almost below my own eyes, all of them now gone past, and some long past, had been thrown open before me as a secret exhibition when first I and they stood within the vestibule of morning hopes,—when the calamities themselves had hardly begun to gather in their elements of possibility, and when some of the parties to them were as yet no more than infants! The past viewed not *as* the past, but by a spectator who steps back ten years deeper into the rear, in order that he may regard it as a future; the calamity of 1840 contemplated from the station of 1830,—the doom that rang the knell of happiness viewed from a point of time when as yet it was neither feared nor would even have been intelligible,—the name that killed in 1843, which in 1835 would have struck no vibration upon the heart, the portrait that on the day of her Majesty's coronation would have been admired by you with a pure disinterested admiration, but which, if seen to-day, would draw forth an involuntary groan,—cases such as these are strangely moving for all who add deep thoughtfulness to deep sensibility. As the hastiest of improvisations, accept, fair reader (for you it is that will chiefly feel such an invocation of the past), three or four illustrations from my own experience.

Who is this distinguished-looking young woman, with her eyes drooping, and the shadow of a dreadful shock yet fresh upon every feature? Who is the elderly lady, with her eyes flashing fire? Who is the downcast child of sixteen? What is that torn paper lying at their feet? Who is the writer? Whom does the paper concern? Ah! if she, if the central figure in the group-twenty-two at the moment when she is revealed to us—could, on her happy birth-day at sweet seventeen, have seen the image of herself five years onwards, just as *we* see it now, would she have prayed for life as for an absolute blessing? or would she not have prayed to be taken from the evil to come—to be taken away one evening, at least, before this day's sun arose? It is true, she still wears a look of gentle pride, and a relic of that noble smile which belongs to *her* that suffers an injury which many times over she would have died sooner than inflict. Womanly pride refuses itself before witnesses to the total prostration of the blow; but, for all *that*, you may see that she longs to be left alone, and that her tears will flow without restraint when she is so. This room is her pretty boudoir, in which, till to-night—poor thing!—she has been glad and happy. There stands her miniature conservatory, and there expands her miniature library; as we circumnavigators of literature are apt (you know) to regard all female libraries in the light of miniatures. None of these will ever rekindle a smile on *her* face; and there, beyond, is her music, which only of all that she possesses will now become dearer to her than ever; but not, as once, to feed a self-mocked pensiveness, or to cheat a half visionary sadness. She will be sad, indeed. But she is one of those that will suffer in silence. Nobody will ever detect *her* failing in any point of duty, or querulously seeking the support in others which she can find for herself in this solitary room. Droop she will not in the sight of men; and, for all beyond, nobody has any concern with that, except God. You shall hear what becomes of her, before we take our departure; but now let me tell you what has happened. In the main outline I am sure you guess already, without aid of mine, for we leaden-eyed men, in such cases, see nothing by comparison with you our quick-witted sisters. That haughty-looking lady, with the Roman cast of features, who must once have been strikingly handsome,—an Agrippina, even yet, in a favorable presentation,- is the younger lady's aunt. She, it is rumored, once sustained, in her younger days, some injury of that same cruel nature which has this day assailed her niece, and ever since she has worn an air of disdain, not altogether unsupported by real dignity towards men. This aunt it was that tore the letter which lies upon the floor. It deserved to be torn; and yet she that had the best right to do so would not have torn it. That letter was an elaborate attempt on the part of an accomplished young man to release himself from sacred engagements. What need was there to argue the case of *such* engagements? Could it have been requisite with pure female dignity to plead anything, or do more than look an indisposition to fulfill them? The aunt is now moving towards the door, which I am glad to see; and she is followed by that pale, timid girl of sixteen, a cousin, who feels the case profoundly, but is too young and shy to offer an intellectual sympathy.

One only person in this world there is who *could* to-night have been a supporting friend to our young sufferer, and *that* is her dear, loving twin-sister, that for eighteen years read and wrote, thought and sang, slept and breathed, with the dividing-door open forever between their bed-rooms, and never once a separation between their hearts; but she is in a far-distant land. Who else is there at her call? Except God, nobody. Her aunt had somewhat sternly admonished her, though still with a relenting in her eye as she glanced aside at the expression in her niece's face, that she must "call-pride to her assistance." Ay, true; but pride, though a strong ally in public, is apt in private to turn as treacherous as the worst of those against whom she is invoked. How could it be dreamed, by a person of sense, that a brilliant young man, of merits various and eminent, in spite of his baseness, to whom, for nearly two years, this young woman had given her whole confiding love, might be dismissed from a heart like hers on the earliest summons of pride, simply because she herself had been dismissed from his, or seemed to have been dismissed, on a summons of mercenary calculation? Look! now that she is relieved from the weight of an unconfidential presence, she has sat for two hours with her head buried in her hands. At last she rises to look for something. A thought has struck her; and, taking a little golden key which hangs by a chain within her bosom, she searches for something locked up amongst her few jewels. What is it? It is a Bible exquisitely illuminated, with a letter attached by some pretty silken artifice to the blank leaves at the end. This letter is a beautiful record, wisely and pathetically composed, of maternal anxiety still burning strong in death, and yearning, when all objects beside were fast fading from *her* eyes, after one parting act of communion with the twin darlings of her heart. Both were thirteen years old, within a week or two, as on the night before her death they sat weeping by the bedside of their mother, and hanging on her lips, now for farewell whispers and now for farewell kisses. They both knew that, as her strength had permitted during the latter month of her life, she had thrown the last anguish of love in her beseeching heart into a letter of counsel to themselves. Through this, of which each sister had a copy, she trusted long to converse with her orphans. And the last promise which she had entreated on this evening from both was, that in either of two contingencies they would review her counsels, and the passages to which she pointed their attention in the Scriptures; namely, first, in the event of any calamity, that, for one sister or for both, should overspread their paths with total darkness; and, secondly, in the event of life flowing in too profound a stream of prosperity, so as to threaten them with an alienation of interest from all spiritual objects. She had riot concealed that, of these two extreme cases, she would prefer for her own children the first. And now had that case arrived, indeed, which she in spirit had desired to meet. Nine years ago, just as the silvery voice of a dial in the dying lady's bed-room was striking nine, upon a summer evening, had the last visual ray streamed from her seeking eyes upon her orphan twins, after which, throughout the night, she had slept away into heaven. Now again had come a summer evening memorable for unhappiness; now again the daughter thought of those dying lights of love which streamed at sunset from the closing eyes of her mother; again, and just as she went back in thought to this image, the same silvery voice of the dial sounded nine o'clock. Again she remembered her mother's dying request; again her own tear-hallowed promise,- and with her heart in her mother's grave she now rose to fulfill it. Here, then, when this solemn recurrence to a testamentary counsel has ceased to be a mere office of duty towards the departed, having taken the shape of a consolation for herself, let us pause.

Now, fair companion in this exploring voyage of inquest into hidden scenes, or forgotten scenes of human life, perhaps it might be instructive to direct our glasses upon the false, perfidious lover. It might. But do not let us do so. We might like him better, or pity him more, than either of us would desire. His name and memory have long since dropped out of everybody's thoughts. Of prosperity, and (what is more important) of internal peace, he is reputed to have had no gleam from the moment when he betrayed his faith, and in one day threw away the jewel of good conscience, and "a pearl richer than all his tribe." But, however that may be, it is certain that, finally, he became a wreck; and of any *hopeless* wreck it is painful to talk,—much more so, when through him others also became wrecks.

Shall we, then, after an interval of nearly two years has passed over the young lady in the boudoir, look in again upon *her*? You hesitate, fair friend; and I myself hesitate. - For in fact she also has become a wreck; and it would grieve us both to see her altered. At the end of twenty-one months she retains hardly a vestige of resemblance to the fine young woman we saw on that unhappy evening, with her aunt and cousin. On consideration, therefore, let us do this. We will direct our glasses to her room at a point of time about six weeks further on. Suppose this time gone; suppose her now dressed for her grave, and placed in her coffin. The advantage of that is, that though no change can restore the ravages of the past, yet (as often is found to happen with young persons) the expression has revived from her girlish years. The child-like aspect has revolved, and settled back upon her features. The wasting away of the flesh is less apparent in the face; and one might imagine that in this sweet marble countenance was seen the very same upon which, eleven years ago, her mother's darkening eyes had lingered to the last, until clouds had swallowed up the vision of her beloved *twins*. Yet, if that were in part a fancy, this, at least, is no fancy,—that not only much of a child-like truth and simplicity has reinstated itself in the temple of her now reposing features, but also that tranquillity and perfect peace, such as are appropriate to eternity, but which from the *living* countenance had taken their flight forever, on that memorable evening when we looked in upon the impassioned group, -upon the towering and denouncing aunt, the sympathizing but silent cousin, the poor, blighted niece, and the wicked letter lying in fragments at their feet.

Cloud, that hast revealed to us this young creature and her blighted hopes, close up again. And now, a few years later,-not more than four or five,-give back to us the latest arrears of the changes which thou concealest within thy draperies. Once more, "open sesame!" and show us a third generation. Behold a lawn islanded with thickets. How perfect is the verdure; how rich the blossoming shrubberies that screen with verdurous walls from the possibility of intrusion, whilst by their own wandering line of distribution they shape, and umbrageously embay, what one might call lawny saloons and vestibules, sylvan galleries and closets! Some of these recesses, which unlink themselves as fluently as snakes, and unexpectedly as the shyest nooks, watery cells, and crypts, amongst the shores of a forest-lake, being formed by the mere caprices and ramblings of the luxuriant shrubs, are so small and so quiet that one might fancy them meant for *boudoirs*. Here is one that in a less fickle climate would make the loveliest of studies for a writer of breathings from some solitary heart, or of *suspiria* from some impassioned memory! And, opening from one angle of this embowered study, issues a little narrow corridor, that, after almost wheeling back upon itself, in its playful mazes, finally widens into a little circular chamber; out of which there is no exit (except back again by the entrance), small or great; so that, adjacent to his study, the writer would command how sweet a bed-room, permitting him to lie the summer through, gazing all night long at the burning host of heaven. How silent *that* would be at the noon of summer nights,—how grave-like in its quiet! And yet, need there be asked a stillness or a silence more profound than is felt at this present noon of day? One reason for such peculiar repose, over and above the tranquil character of the day, and the distance of the place from the highroads, is the outer zone of woods, which almost on every quarter invests the shrubberies, swathing them (as one may express it), belting them and overlooking them, from a varying distance of two and three furlongs, so as oftentimes to keep the winds at a distance. But, however caused and supported, the silence of these fanciful lawns and lawny chambers is oftentimes oppressive in the depths of summer to people unfamiliar with solitudes, either mountainous or sylvan; and many would be apt to suppose that the villa, to which these pretty shrubberies form the chief dependencies, must be untenanted. But that is not the case. The house is inhabited, and by its own legal mistress, the proprietress of the whole domain; and not at all a silent mistress, but as noisy as most little ladies of five years old, for that is her age. Now, and just as we are speaking, you may hear her little joyous clamor, as she issues from the house. This way she comes, bounding like a fawn; and soon she rushes into the little recess which I pointed out as a proper study for any man who should be weaving the deep harmonies of memorial *suspiria*. But I fancy that she will soon dispossess it of that character, for her *suspiria* are not many at this stage of her life. Now she comes dancing into sight; and you see that, if she keeps the promise of her infancy, she will be an interesting creature to the eye in after life. In other respects, also, she is an engaging child,—loving, natural, and wild as any one of her neighbors for some miles round, namely, leverets, squirrels, and ring-doves. But what will surprise you most is, that, although a child of pure English blood, she speaks very little English; but more Bengalee than perhaps you will find it convenient to construe. That is her ayah, who comes up from behind, at a pace so different from her youthful mistress's. But, if their paces are different, in other things they agree most cordially; and dearly they love each other. In reality, the child has passed her whole life in the arms of this ayah. She remembers nothing elder than *her*; eldest of things is the ayah in her eyes; and, if the ayah should insist on her worshipping herself as the goddess Railroadina or Steamboatina, that made England, and the sea, and Bengal, it is certain that the little thing would do so, asking no question but this,—whether kissing would do for worshipping.

Every evening at nine o'clock; as the ayah sits by the little creature lying awake in bed, the silvery tongue of a dial tolls the hour. Reader, you know who she is. She is the grand-daughter of her that faded away about sunset in gazing at her twin orphans. Her name is Grace. And she is the niece of that elder and once happy Grace; who spent so much of her happiness in this, very room, but whom, in her utter desolation, we saw in the boudoir, with the torn letter at her feet. She is the daughter of that other sister, wife to a military officer who died abroad. Little Grace never saw her grandmamma, nor her lovely aunt, that was her namesake, nor consciously her mamma. She was born six months after the death of the elder Grace; and her mother saw her only through the mists of mortal suffering, which carried her off three weeks after the birth of her daughter.

This view was taken several years ago; and since then the younger Grace, in her turn, is under a cloud of affliction. But she is still under eighteen; and of her there may be hopes. Seeing such things in so short a space of years, for the grandmother died at. thirty-two, we say,—Death we can face: but knowing, as some of us do, what is human life, which of us is it that without shuddering could (if consciously we were summoned) face the hour of birth?

THE ENGLISH MAIL-COACH;

OR, THE GLORY OF MOTION

SOME twenty or more years before I matriculated at Oxford, Mr. Palmer, M. P. for Bath, had accomplished two things, very hard to do on our little planet, the Earth, however cheap they may happen to be held by the eccentric people in comets: he had invented mail-coaches, and he had married the daughter [34] of a duke. He was, therefore, just twice as great a man as Galileo, who certainly invented (or *discovered*) the satellites of Jupiter, those very next things extant to mail-coaches in the two capital points of speed and keeping time, but who did not marry the daughter of a duke.

[34] Lady Madeline Gordon.

These mail-coaches, as organized by Mr. Palmer, are entitled to a circumstantial notice from myself having had so large a share in developing the anarchies of my subsequent dreams, an agency which they accomplished, first, through velocity, at that time unprecedented; they first revealed the glory of motion: suggesting, at the same time, an under-sense, not unpleasurable, of possible though indefinite danger; secondly, through grand effects for the eye between. lamp-light and the darkness upon solitary roads; thirdly, through animal beauty and power so often displayed in the class of horses selected for this mail service; fourthly, through the conscious presence of a central intellect, that, in the midst of vast distances [35] , of storms, of darkness, of night, overruled all obstacles into one steady cooperation in a national result. To my own feeling, this post-office service recalled some mighty orchestra, where a thousand instruments, all disregarding each other, and so far in danger of discord, yet all obedient as slaves to the supreme *baton* of some great leader, terminate in a perfection of harmony like that of heart, veins, and arteries, in a healthy animal organization. But, finally, that particular element in this whole combination which most impressed myself, and through which it is that to this hour Mr. Palmer's mail-coach system tyrannizes by terror and terrific beauty over my dreams, lay in the awful political mission which at that time it fulfilled. The mail-coaches it was that distributed over the face of the land, like the opening of apocalyptic vials, the heart-shaking news of Trafalgar, of Salamanca, of Vittoria, of Waterloo. These were the harvests that, in the grandeur of their reaping, redeemed the tears and blood in which they had been sown. Neither was the meanest peasant so much below the grandeur and the sorrow of the times as to confound these battles, which were gradually moulding the destinies of Christendom, with the vulgar conflicts of ordinary warfare, which are oftentimes but gladiatorial trials of national prowess. The victories of England in this stupendous contest rose of themselves as natural *Te Deums* to heaven;. and it was felt by the thoughtful that such victories, at such a crisis of general prostration, were not more beneficial to ourselves than finally to France, and to the nations of western and central Europe, through whose pusillanimity it was that the French domination had prospered.

[35] "*Vast distances*."—One case was familiar to mail-coach travellers, where two mails in opposite directions, north and south, starting at the same minute from points six hundred miles apart, met almost constantly at a particular bridge which exactly

bisected the total distance.

The mail-coach, as the national organ for publishing these mighty events, became itself a spiritualized and glorified object to an impassioned heart; and naturally, in the Oxford of that day, all hearts were awakened. There were, perhaps, of us gownsmen, two thousand *resident* [36] in Oxford, and dispersed through five-and-twenty colleges. In some of these the custom permitted the student to keep what are called 'short terms;' that is, the four terms of Michaelmas, Lent, Easter, and Act, were kept severally by a residence, in the aggregate, of ninety-one days, or thirteen weeks. Under this interrupted residence, accordingly, it was possible that a student might have a reason for going down to his home four times in the year. This made eight journeys to and fro. And as these homes lay dispersed through all the shires of the island, and most of us disdained all coaches except his majesty's mail, no city out of London could pretend to so extensive a connection with Mr. Palmer's establishment as Oxford. Naturally, therefore, it became a point of some interest with us, whose journeys revolved every six weeks on an average, to look a little into the executive details of the system. With some of these Mr. Palmer had no concern; they rested upon bye-laws not unreasonable, enacted by posting-houses for their own benefit, and upon others equally stern, enacted by the inside passengers for the illustration of their own exclusiveness. These last were of a nature to rouse our scorn, from which the transition was not very long to mutiny. Up to this time, it had been the fixed assumption of the four inside people, (as an old tradition of all public carriages from the reign of Charles II.,) that they, the illustrious quaternion, constituted a porcelain variety of the human race, whose dignity would have been compromised by exchanging one word of civility with the three miserable delf ware outsides. Even to have kicked an outsider might have been held to attaint the foot concerned in that operation; so that, perhaps, it would have required an act of parliament to restore its purity of blood. What words, then, could express the horror, and the sense of treason, in that case, which *had* happened, where all three outsides, the trinity of Pariahs, made a vain attempt to sit down at the same breakfast table or dinner table with the consecrated four? I myself witnessed such an attempt; and on that occasion a benevolent old gentleman endeavored to soothe his three holy associates, by suggesting that, if the outsides were indicted for this criminal attempt at the next assizes, the court would regard it as a case of lunacy (or *delirium tremens*) rather than of treason. England owes much of her grandeur to the depth of the aristocratic element in her social composition. I am not the man to laugh at it. But sometimes it expressed itself in extravagant shapes. The course taken with the infatuated outsiders, in the particular attempt which I have noticed, was, that the waiter, beckoning them away from the privileged *sale à manger*, sang out, 'This way, my good men;' and then enticed them away off to the kitchen. But that plan had not always answered. Sometimes, though very rarely, cases occurred where the intruders, being stronger than usual, or more vicious than usual, resolutely refused to move, and so far carried their point, as to have a separate table arranged for themselves in a corner of the room. Yet, if an Indian screen could be found ample enough to plant them out from the very eyes of the high table, or *dais*, it then became possible to assume as a fiction of law that the three delf fellows, after all, were not present. They could be ignored by the porcelain men, under the maxim, that objects not appearing, and not existing, are governed by the same logical construction.

[36] "*Resident*."—The number on the books was far greater, many of whom kept up an

intermitting communication with Oxford. But I speak of those only who were steadily pursuing their academic studies, and of those who resided constantly as *fellows*.

Such now being, at that time, the usages of mail-coaches, what was to be done by us of young Oxford? We, the most aristocratic of people, who were addicted to the practice of looking down superciliously even upon the insides themselves as often very suspicious characters, were we voluntarily to court indignities? If our dress and bearing sheltered us, generally, from the suspicion of being 'raff,' (the name at that period for 'snobs,' [37]) we really *were* such constructively, by the place we assumed. If we did not submit to the deep shadow of eclipse, we entered at least the skirts of its penumbra. And the analogy of theatres was urged against us, where no man can complain of the annoyances incident to the pit or gallery, having his instant remedy in paying the higher price of the boxes. But the soundness of this analogy we disputed. In the case of the theatre, it cannot be pretended that the inferior situations have any separate attractions, unless the pit suits the purpose of the dramatic reporter. But the reporter or critic is a rarity. For most people, the sole benefit is in the price. Whereas, on the contrary, the outside of the mail had its own incommunicable advantages. These we could not forego. The higher price we should willingly have paid, but *that* was connected with the condition of riding inside, which was insufferable. The air, the freedom of prospect, the proximity to the horses, the elevation of seat—these were what we desired; but above all, the certain anticipation of purchasing occasional opportunities of driving.

[37] "Snobs," and its antithesis, "nobs," arose among the internal factions of shoe-makers perhaps ten years later. Possibly enough, the terms may have existed much earlier; but they were then first made known, picturesquely and effectively, by a trial at some assizes which happened to fix the public attention.

Under coercion of this great practical difficulty, we instituted a searching inquiry into the true quality and valuation of the different apartments about the mail. We conducted this inquiry on metaphysical principles; and it was ascertained satisfactorily, that the roof of the coach, which some had affected to call the attics, and some the garrets, was really the drawing-room, and the box was the chief ottoman or sofa in that drawing-room; whilst it appeared that the inside, which had been traditionally regarded as the only room tenantable by gentlemen, was, in fact, the coal-cellar in disguise.

Great wits jump: The very same idea had not long before struck the celestial intellect of China. Amongst the presents carried out by our first embassy to that country was a state-coach. It had been specially selected as a personal gift by George III.; but the exact mode of using it was a mystery to Pekin. The ambassador, indeed, (Lord Maccartney,) had made some dim and imperfect explanations upon the point; but as his excellency communicated these in a diplomatic whisper, at the very moment of his departure, the celestial mind was very feebly illuminated; and it became necessary to call a cabinet council on the grand state question—'Where was the emperor to sit?' The hammer-cloth happened to be unusually gorgeous; and partly on that consideration, but partly also because the box offered the most elevated seat, and undeniably went foremost, it was resolved by acclamation that the box was the imperial place, and, *for the scoundrel who drove, he might sit where lie could find a perch.* The horses, therefore, being harnessed, under a flourish of music and a salute of guns, solemnly his imperial majesty ascended his new English throne, having the first lord of the treasury on his right hand, and the chief jester on his left. Pekin gloried in the spectacle; and in the whole flowery people, constructively present by representation, there was but one discontented person, which was the coachman. This mutinous individual, looking as black-hearted as he really was, audaciously shouted, 'Where am *I* to sit?' But the privy council, incensed by his disloyalty, unanimously opened the door, and kicked him into the inside. He had all the inside places to himself; but such is the rapacity of ambition, that he was still dissatisfied. 'I say,' he cried out in an extempore petition, addressed to the emperor through the window, 'how am I to catch hold of the reins?' 'Any how,' was the answer;' don't trouble *me*, man, in my glory; through the windows, through the key-holes—how you please.' Finally this contumacious coachman lengthened the check-strings into a sort of jury-reins, communicating with the horses; with these he drove as steadily as may be supposed. The emperor returned after the briefest of circuits; he. descended in great pomp from his throne, with the severest resolution never to remount it. A public thanksgiving was ordered for his majesty's prosperous escape from the disease of a broken neck; and the state-coach was dedicated for ever as a votive offering to the god Fo, Fo—whom the learned more accurately called Fi, Fi.

A revolution of this same Chinese character did young Oxford of that era effect in the constitution of mail-coach society. It was a perfect French revolution; and we had good reason to say, *Ca ira*. In fact, it soon became too popular. The 'public,' a well known character, particularly disagreeable, though slightly respectable, and notorious for affecting the chief seats in synagogues, had at first loudly opposed this revolution; but when the opposition showed itself to be ineffectual, our disagreeable friend went into it with headlong zeal. At first it was a sort of race between us; and, as the public is usually above thirty, (say generally from thirty to fifty years old,) naturally we of young Oxford, that averaged about twenty, had the advantage. Then the public took to bribing, giving fees to horse-keepers, &c., who hired out their persons as warming-pans on the box-seat. *That*, you know, was shocking to our moral sensibilities. Come to bribery, we observed, and there is an end to all morality, Aristotle's, Cicero's, or anybody's. And, besides, of what use was it? For *we* bribed also. And as our bribes to those of the public being demonstrated out of Euclid to be as five shillings to sixpence, here again young Oxford had the advantage. But the contest was ruinous to the principles of the stable establishment about the mails. The whole corporation was constantly bribed, rebribed, and often sur-rebribed; so that a horse-keeper, ostler, or helper, was held by the philosophical at that time to be the most corrupt character in the nation.

There was an impression upon the public mind, natural enough from the continually augmenting velocity of the mail, but quite erroneous, that an outside seat on this class of carriages was a post of danger. On the contrary, I maintained that, if a man had become nervous from some gipsy prediction in his childhood, allocating to a particular moon now approaching some unknown danger, and he should inquire earnestly, 'Whither can I go for shelter? Is a prison the safest retreat? Or a lunatic hospital? Or the British Museum?' I should have replied,' Oh, no; I'll tell you what to do. Take lodgings for the next forty days on the box of his majesty's mail. Nobody can touch you there. If it is by bills at ninety days after date that you are made unhappy—if noters and protesters are the sort of wretches whose astrological shadows darken the house of life—then note you what I vehemently protest, viz., that no matter though the sheriff in every county should be running after you with his posse, touch a hair of your head he cannot whilst you keep house, and have your legal domicile on the box of the mail. It's felony to stop the mail;

even the sheriff cannot do that. And an *extra* (no great matter if it grazes the sheriff) touch of the whip to the leaders at any time guarantees your safety.' In fact, a bedroom in a quiet house, seems a safe enough retreat; yet it is liable to its own notorious nuisances, to robbers by night, to rats, to fire. But the mail laughs. at these terrors. To robbers, the answer is packed up and ready for delivery in the barrel of the guard's blunderbuss. Rats again! there *are* none about mail-coaches, any more than snakes in Van Troil's Iceland; except, indeed, now and then a parliamentary rat, who always hides his shame in the 'coal cellar.' And, as to fire, I never knew but one in a mail-coach, which was in the Exeter mail, and caused by an obstinate sailor bound to Davenport. Jack, making light of the law and the lawgiver that had set their faces against his offence, insisted on taking up a forbidden seat in the rear of the roof, from which he could exchange his own yarns with those of the guard. No greater offence was then known to mail-coaches; it was treason, it was *laesa majestas*, it was by tendency arson; and the ashes of Jack's pipe, falling amongst the straw of the hinder boot, containing the mail-bags, raised a flame which (aided by the wind of our motion) threatened a revolution in the republic of letters. But even this left the sanctity of the box unviolated. In dignified repose, the coachman and myself sat on, resting with benign composure upon our knowledge—that the fire would have to burn its way through four inside passengers before it could reach ourselves. With a quotation rather too trite, I remarked to the coachman,—

> —"Jam proximus ardet
> Ucalegon."

But, recollecting that the Virgilian part of his education might have been neglected, I interpreted so far as to say, that perhaps at that moment the flames were catching hold of our worthy brother and next-door neighbor Ucalegon. The coachman said nothing, but, by his faint sceptical smile, he seemed to be thinking that he knew better; for that in fact, Ucalegon, as it happened, was not in the way-bill.

No dignity is perfect which does not at some point ally itself with the indeterminate and mysterious. The connection of the mail with the state and the executive government a connection obvious, but yet not strictly defined—gave to the whole mail establishment a grandeur and an official authority which did us service on the roads, and invested us with seasonable terrors. But perhaps these terrors were not the less impressive, because their exact legal limits were imperfectly ascertained. Look at those turnpike gates; with what deferential hurry, with what an obedient start, they fly open at. our approach! Look at that long line of carts and carters ahead, audaciously usurping the very crest of the road. All! traitors, they do not hear us as yet; but as soon as the dreadful blast of our horn reaches them with the proclamation of our approach, see with what frenzy of trepidation they fly to their horses' heads, and deprecate our wrath by the precipitation of their crane-neck quarterings. Treason they feel to be their crime; each individual carter feels himself under the ban of confiscation and attainder: his blood is attainted through six generations, and nothing is wanting but the headsman and his axe, the block and the sawdust, to close up the vista of his horrors. What! shall it be within benefit of clergy to delay the king's message on the high road?—to interrupt the great respirations, ebb or flood, of the national intercourse—to endanger the safety of tidings, running day and night between all nations and languages? Or can it be fancied, amongst the weakest of men, that the bodies of the criminals will be given up to their widows for Christian burial? Now the doubts which were raised as to our powers did more to wrap them in terror, by wrapping them in uncertainty, than could have been effected by the sharpest definitions of the law from the Quarter Sessions. We, on our parts, (we, the collective mail, I mean,) did our utmost to exalt the idea of our privileges by the insolence with which we wielded them. Whether this insolence rested upon law that gave it a sanction, or upon conscious power, haughtily dispensing with that sanction, equally it spoke from a potential station; and the agent in each particular insolence of the moment, was viewed reverentially, as one having authority.

Sometimes after breakfast his majesty's mail would become frisky: and in its difficult wheelings amongst the intricacies of early markets, it would upset an apple cart, a cart loaded with eggs, &c. Huge was the affliction and dismay, awful was the smash, though, after all, I believe the damage might be levied upon the hundred. I, as far as possible, endeavored in such a case to represent the conscience and moral sensibilities of the mail; and, when wildernesses of eggs were lying poached under our horses' hoofs, then would I stretch forth my hands in sorrow, saying (in words too celebrated in those days from the false [38] echoes of Marengo)—'Ah! wherefore have we not time to weep over you?' which was quite impossible, for in fact we had not even time to laugh over them. Tied to post-office time, with an allowance in some cases of fifty minutes for eleven miles, could the royal mail pretend to undertake the offices of sympathy and condolence? Could it be expected to provide tears for the accidents of the road? If even it seemed to trample on humanity, it did so, I contended, in discharge of its own more peremptory duties.

[38] "False echoes"—yes, false! for the words ascribed to Napoleon, as breathed to the memory of Desaix, never were uttered at all. They stand in the same category of theatrical inventions as the cry of the foundering *Vengeur*, as the vaunt of General Cambronne at Waterloo, "*La Garde meurt, mais ne se rend pas*," as the repartees of Talleyrand.

Upholding the morality of the mail, *à fortiori* I upheld its rights, I stretched to the uttermost its privilege of imperial precedency, and astonished weak minds by the feudal powers which I hinted to be lurking constructively in the charters of this proud establishment. Once I remember being on the box of the Holyhead mail, between Shrewsbury and Oswestry, when a tawdry thing from Birmingham, some *Tallyho* or *Highflier*, all flaunting with green and gold, came up alongside of us. What a contrast to our royal simplicity of form and color is this plebeian wretch! The single ornament on our dark ground of chocolate color was the mighty shield of the imperial arms, but emblazoned in proportions as modest as a signet-ring bears to a seal of office. Even this was displayed only on a single panel, whispering, rather than proclaiming, our relations to the state; whilst the beast from Birmingham had as much writing and painting on its sprawling flanks as would have puzzled a decipherer from the tombs of Luxor. For some time this Birmingham machine ran along by our side—a piece of familiarity that seemed to us sufficiently jacobinical. But all at once a movement of the horses announced a desperate intention of leaving us behind. 'Do you see *that*?' I said to the coachman.' I see,' was his short answer. He was awake, yet he waited longer than seemed prudent; for the horses of our audacious opponent had a disagreeable air of freshness and power. But his motive was loyal; his wish was that the Birmingham conceit should be full-blown before he froze it. When *that* seemed right, he unloosed, or, to speak by a stronger image, he sprang his known resources, he slipped our royal horses like cheetahs, or hunting leopards, after the affrighted game. How they could retain such a reserve of fiery power after the work they had accomplished, seemed hard to explain. But on our side, besides the physical superiority, was a tower of strength, namely, the king's name, 'which they upon the adverse faction wanted.' Passing them without an effort, as it seemed, we threw them into the rear with so lengthening an interval between us, as proved in itself the bitterest mockery of their presumption; whilst our guard blew back a shattering blast of triumph, that was really too painfully full of derision.

I mention this little incident for its connection with what followed. A Welshman, sitting behind me, asked if I had not felt my heart burn within me during the continuance of the race? I said - no; because we were not racing with a mail, so that no glory could be gained. In fact, it was sufficiently mortifying that such a Birmingham thing should dare to challenge us. The Welshman replied, that he didn't see *that*; for that a cat might look at a king, and a Brummagem coach might lawfully race the Holyhead mail. '*Race* us perhaps,' I replied,' though even *that* has an air of sedition, but not *beat* us. This would have been treason; and for its own sake I am glad that the Tallyho vas disappointed.' So dissatisfied did the Welshman seem with this opinion, that at last I was obliged to tell him a very fine story from one of our elder dramatists, viz.- that once, in some oriental region, when the prince of all the land, with his splendid court, were flying their falcons, a hawk suddenly flew at a majestic eagle; and in defiance of the eagle's prodigious advantages, in sight also of all the astonished field sportsmen, spectators, and followers, killed him on the spot. The prince was struck with amazement at the unequal contest, and with burning admiration for its unparalleled result. He commanded that the hawk should be brought before him; caressed the bird with enthusiasm, and ordered that, for the commemoration of his matchless courage, a crown of gold should be solemnly placed on the hawk's head; but then that, immediately after this coronation, the bird should be led off to execution, as the most valiant indeed of traitors, but not the less a traitor that had dared to rise in rebellion against his liege lord the eagle. 'Now,' said I to the Welshman, 'how painful it would have been to you and me as men of refined feelings, that this poor brute, the Tallyho, in the impossible case of a victory over us, should have been crowned with jewellery, gold, with Birmingham ware, or paste diamonds, and then led off to instant execution.' The Welshman doubted if that could be warranted by law. And when I hinted at the 10th of Edward III., chap. 15, for regulating the precedency of coaches, as being probably the statute relied on for the capital punishment of such offences, he replied drily—that if the attempt to pass a mail was really treasonable, it was a pity that the Tallyho appeared to have so imperfect an acquaintance with law.

These were among the gaieties of my earliest and boyish acquaintance with mails. But alike the gayest and the most terrific of my experiences rose again after years of slumber, armed with preternatural power to shake my dreaming sensibilities; sometimes, as in the slight case of Miss Fanny on the Bath road, (which I will immediately mention,) through some casual or capricious association with images originally gay, yet opening at some stage of evolution into sudden capacities of horror; sometimes through the more natural and fixed alliances with the sense of power so various lodged in the mail system.

The modern modes of travelling cannot compare with the mail-coach system in grandeur and power. They boast of more velocity, but not however as a consciousness, but as a fact of our lifeless knowledge, resting upon *alien* evidence; as, for instance, because somebody *says* that we have gone fifty miles in the hour, or upon the evidence of a result, as that actually we find ourselves in York four hours after leaving London. Apart from such an assertion, or such a result, I am little aware of the pace. But, seated on the old mail-coach, we needed no evidence out of ourselves to indicate the velocity. On this system the word was- *Non magna loquimur*, as upon railways, but *magna vivimus*. The vital experience of the glad animal sensibilities made doubts impossible on the question of our speed; we heard our speed, we saw it, we felt it as a thrilling; and this speed was not the product of blind insensate agencies, that had no sympathy to give, but was incarcerated in the fiery eyeballs of an animal, in his dilated nostril, spasmodic muscles, and echoing hoofs. This speed was incarnated in the visible contagion amongst brutes of some impulse, that, radiating into their natures, had yet its centre and beginning in man. The sensibility of the horse, uttering itself in the maniac light of his eye, might be the last vibration of such a movement; the glory of Salamanca might be the first—but the intervening link that connected them, that spread the earthquake of the battle into the eyeball of the horse, was the heart of man —kindling in the rapture of the fiery strife, and then propagating its own tumults by motions and gestures to the sympathies, more or less dim, in his servant the horse.

But now, on the new system of travelling, iron tubes and boilers have disconnected man's heart from the ministers of his locomotion. Nile nor Trafalgar has power any more to raise an extra bubble in a steam-kettle. The galvanic cycle is broken up for ever; man's imperial nature no longer sends itself forward through the electric sensibility of the horse; the interagencies are gone in the mode of communication between the horse and his master, out of which grew so many aspects of sublimity under accidents of mists that hid, or sudden blazes that revealed, of mobs that agitated, or midnight solitudes that awed. Tidings, fitted to convulse all nations, must henceforwards travel by culinary process; and the trumpet that once announced from afar the laurelled mail, heart-shaking, when heard screaming on the wind, and advancing through the darkness to every village or solitary house on its route, has now given way for ever to the pot-wallopings of the boiler.

Thus have perished multiform openings for sublime effects, for interesting personal communications, for revelations of impressive faces that could not have offered themselves amongst the hurried and fluctuating groups of a railway station. The gatherings of gazers about a mail-coach had one centre, and acknowledged only one interest. But the crowds attending at a railway station have as little unity as running water, and own as many centres as there are separate carriages in the train.

How else, for example, than as a constant watcher for the dawn, and for the London mail that in summer months entered about dawn into the lawny thickets of Marlborough Forest, couldst thou, sweet Fanny of the Bath road, have become known to myself? Yet Fanny, as the loveliest young woman for face and person that perhaps in my whole life I have beheld, merited the station which even her I could not willingly have spared; yet (thirty-five years later) she holds in my dreams; and though, by an accident of fanciful caprice, she brought along with her into those dreams a troop of dreadful creatures, fabulous and not fabulous, that were more abominable to a human heart than Fanny and the dawn were delightful, *her* I could not willingly have spared.

Miss Fanny of the Bath road, strictly speaking, lived at a mile's distance from that road, but came so continually to meet the mail, that I on my frequent transits rarely missed her, and naturally connected her name with the great thoroughfare where I saw her; I do not exactly know, but I believe with some burthen of commissions to be executed in Bath, her own residence being probably the centre to which these commissions gathered. The mail coachman, who wore the royal livery, being one amongst the privileged few [39], happened to be Fanny's grandfather. A good man he was, that loved his beautiful granddaughter; and, loving her wisely, was vigilant over her deportment in any case where young Oxford might happen to be concerned. Was I then vain enough to imagine that I myself, individually, could fall within the line of his terrors? Certainly not, as regarded any physical pretensions that I could plead; for Fanny (as a chance passenger from her own neighborhood once told me) counted in her train a hundred and ninety-nine professed admirers, if not open aspirants to her favor; and probably not one of the whole brigade but excelled myself in personal advantages. Ulysses even, with the unfair advantage of his accursed bow, could hardly have undertaken that amount of suitors. So the danger might have seemed slight—only that woman is universally aristocratic; it is amongst her nobilities of heart that she is so. Now, the aristocratic distinctions in my favor might easily with Miss Fanny have compensated my physical deficiencies. Did I then make love to Fanny? Why, yes; *mais oui donc*; as much love as one can make whilst the mail is changing horses, a process which ten years later did not occupy above eighty seconds; but *then*, viz., about Waterloo, it occupied five times eighty. Now, four hundred seconds offer a field quite ample enough for whispering into a young woman's ear a great deal of truth; and (by way of parenthesis) some trifle of falsehood. Grandpapa did right, therefore, to watch me. And yet, as happens too often to the grandpapas of earth, in a contest with the admirers of granddaughters, how vainly would he have watched me had I meditated any evil whispers to Fanny! She, it is my belief, would have protected herself against any man's evil suggestions. But he, as the result showed, could not have intercepted the opportunities for such suggestions. Yet he was still active; he was still blooming. Blooming he was as Fanny herself.

"Say, all our praises why should lords—"

No, that's not the line.

"Say, all our roses why should girls engross?"

The coachman showed rosy blossoms on his face deeper even than his granddaughter's,—his being drawn from the ale cask, Fanny's from youth and innocence, and from the fountains of the dawn. But, in spite of his blooming face, some infirmities he had; and one particularly (am very sure no *more* than one,) in which he too much resembled a crocodile. This lay in a monstrous inaptitude for turning round. The crocodile, I presume, owes that inaptitude to the absurd *length* of his back; but in our grandpapa it arose rather from the absurd *breadth* of his back, combined, probably, with some growing stiffness in his legs. Now upon this crocodile infirmity of his I planted an easy opportunity for tendering my homage to Miss Fanny. In defiance of all his honorable vigilance, no sooner had he presented to us his mighty Jovian back (what a field for displaying to mankind his royal scarlet!) whilst inspecting professionally the buckles, the straps, and the silver turrets of his harness, than I raised Miss Fanny's hand to my lips, and, by the mixed tenderness and respectfulness of my manner, caused her easily to understand how happy it would have made me to rank upon her list as No. 10 or 12, in which case a few casualties amongst her lovers (and observe—they *hanged* liberally in those days) might have promoted me speedily to the top of the tree; as, on the other hand, with how much loyalty of submission I acquiesced in her allotment, supposing that she had seen reason to plant me in the very rearward of her favor, as No. 199+1. It must not be supposed that I allowed any trace of jest, or even of playfulness, to mingle with these expressions of my admiration; that would have been insulting to her, and would have been false as regarded my own feelings. In fact, the utter shadowyness of our relations to each other, even after our meetings through seven or eight years had been very numerous, but of necessity had been very brief, being entirely on mail-coach allowance—timed, in reality, by the General Post Office— and watched by a crocodile belonging to the antepenultimate generation, left it easy for me to do a thing which few people ever *can* have done—viz., to make love for seven years, at the same time to be as sincere as ever creature was, and yet never to compromise myself by overtures that might have been foolish as regarded my own interests, or misleading as regarded hers. Most truly I loved this beautiful and ingenuous girl; and had it not been for the Bath and Bristol mail, heaven only knows what might have come of it. People talk of being over head and ears in love—now, the mail was the cause that I sank only over ears in love, which, you know, still left a trifle of brain to overlook the whole conduct of the affair. I have not mentioned the case at all for the sake of a dreadful result from it in after years of dreaming. But it seems, *ex abundanti*, to yield this moral—viz., that as, in England, the idiot and the half-wit are held to be under the guardianship of chancery, so the man making love, who is often but a variety of the same imbecile class, ought to be made a ward of the General Post-Office, whose severe course of *timing* and periodical interruption might intercept many a foolish declaration, such as lays a solid foundation for fifty years' repentance.

[39] "Privileged few." The general impression was that this splendid costume belonged of right to the mail coachmen as their professional dress. But that was an error. To the guard it *did* belong as a matter of course, and was essential as an official warrant, and a means of instant identification for his person, in the discharge of his important public duties. but the coachman, and especially if his place in the series did not connect him immediately with London and the General Post Office, obtained the scarlet coat only as an honorary distinction after long or special service.

Ah, reader! when I look back upon those days, it seems to me that all things change or perish. Even thunder and lightning, it pains me to say, are not the thunder and lightning which I seem to remember about the time of Waterloo. Roses, I fear, are degenerating, and, without a Red revolution, must come to the dust. The Fannies of our island —though this I say with reluctance —are not improving; and the Bath road is notoriously superannuated. Mr. Waterton tells me that the crocodile does *not* change — that a cayman, in fact, or an alligator, is just as good for riding upon as he was in the time of the Pharaohs. *That* may be; but the reason is, that the crocodile does not live fast—he is a slow coach. I believe it is generally understood amongst naturalists, that the crocodile is a blockhead. It is my own impression that the Pharaohs were also blockheads. Now, as the Pharaohs and the crocodile domineered over Egyptian society, this accounts for a singular mistake that prevailed on the Nile. The crocodile made the ridiculous blunder of supposing man to be meant chiefly for his own eating. Man, taking a different view of the subject, naturally met that mistake by another; he viewed the crocodile as a thing sometimes to worship, but always to run away from. And this continued until Mr. Waterton changed the relations between the animals. The mode of escaping from the reptile he showed to be, not by running away, but by leaping on its back, booted and spurred. The two animals had misunderstood each other. The use of the crocodile has now been cleared up—it is to be ridden; and the use of man is, that he may improve the health of the crocodile by riding him a fox-hunting before breakfast. And it is pretty certain that any crocodile, who has been regularly hunted through the season, and is master of the weight he carries, will take a six-barred gate now as well as ever he would have done in the infancy of the pyramids.

Perhaps, therefore, the crocodile does *not* change, but all things else *do*: even the shadow of the pyramids grows less. And often the restoration in vision of Fanny and the Bath road, makes me too pathetically sensible of that truth. Out of the darkness, if I happen to call up the image of Fanny from thirty-five years back, arises suddenly a rose in June; or, if I think for an instant of the rose in June, up rises the heavenly face of Fanny. One after the other, like the antiphonies in the choral service, rises Fanny and the rose in June, then back again the rose in June and Fanny. Then come both together, as in a chorus; roses and Fannies, Fannies and roses, without end — thick as blossoms in paradise. Then comes a venerable crocodile, in a royal livery of scarlet and gold, or in a coat with sixteen capes; and the crocodile is driving four-in-hand from the box of the Bath mail. And suddenly we upon the mail are pulled up by a mighty dial, sculptured with the hours, and with the dreadful legend of TOO LATE. Then all at once we are arrived at Marlborough forest, amongst the lovely households [40] of the roe-deer: these retire into the dewy thickets; the thickets are rich with roses; the roses call up (as ever) the sweet countenance of Fanny, who, being the granddaughter of a crocodile, awakens a dreadful host of wild semi-legendary animals, — griffins, dragons, basilisks, sphinxes,- till at length the whole vision of fighting images crowds into one towering armorial shield, a vast emblazonry of human charities and human loveliness that have perished, but quartered heraldically with unutterable horrors of monstrous and demoniac natures, whilst over all rises, as a surmounting crest, one fair female hand, with the fore-finger pointing, in sweet, sorrowful admonition, upwards to heaven, and having power (which, without experience, I never could have believed) to awaken the pathos that kills in the very bosom of the horrors that madden the grief that gnaws at the heart, together with the monstrous creations of darkness that shock the belief, and make dizzy the reason of man. This is the peculiarity that I wish the reader to notice, as having first been made known to me for a possibility by this early vision of Fanny on the Bath road. The peculiarity consisted in the confluence of two different keys, though apparently repelling each other, into the music and governing principles of the same dream; horror, such as possesses the maniac, and yet, by momentary transitions, grief, such as may be supposed to possess the dying mother when leaving her infant children to the mercies of the cruel. Unusually, and perhaps always, in an unshaken nervous system, these two modes of misery exclude each other — here first they met in horrid reconciliation. There was also a separate peculiarity in the quality of the horror. This was afterwards developed into far more revolting complexities of misery and incomprehensible darkness; and perhaps I am wrong in ascribing any value as a *causative* agency to this particular case on the Bath road — possibly it furnished merely an *occasion* that accidentally introduced a mode of horrors certain, at any rate, to have grown up, with or without the Bath road, from more advanced stages of the nervous derangement. Yet, as the cubs of tigers or leopards, when domesticated, have been observed to suffer a sudden development of their latent ferocity under too eager an appeal to their playfulness —the gaieties of sport in them being too closely connected with the fiery brightness of their murderous instincts—so I have remarked that the caprices, the gay arabesques, and the lovely floral luxuriations of dreams, betray a shocking tendency to pass into finer maniacal splendors. That gaiety, for instance, (for such at first it was,) in the dreaming faculty, by which one principal point of resemblance to a crocodile in the mail-coachman was soon made to clothe him with the form of a crocodile, and yet was blended with accessory circumstances derived from his *human* functions, passed rapidly into a further development, no longer gay or playful, but. terrific, the most terrific that besieges dreams, viz.—the horrid inoculation upon each other of incompatible natures. This horror has always been secretly felt by man; it was felt even under pagan forms of religion, which offered a very feeble, and also a very limited gamut for giving expression to the human capacities of sublimity or of horror. We read it in the fearful composition of the sphinx. The dragon, again, is the snake inoculated upon the scorpion. The basilisk unites the mysterious malice of the evil eye, unintentional on the part of the unhappy agent, with the intentional venom of some other malignant natures. But these horrid complexities of evil agency are but *objectively* horrid; they inflict the horror suitable to their compound nature; but there is no insinuation that they feel that horror.' Heraldry is so full of these fantastic creatures, that, in some zoologies, we find a separate chapter or a supplement dedicated to what is denominated heraldic zoology. And why not? For these hideous creatures, however visionary [41], have a real traditionary ground in medieval belief—sincere and partly reasonable, though adulterating with mendacity, blundering, credulity, and intense superstition. But the dream-horror which I speak of, is far more frightful. The dreamer finds housed within himself- occupying, as it were, some separate chamber in his brain—holding, perhaps, from that station a secret and detestable commerce with his own heart—some horrid alien nature. What if it were his own nature repeated, — still, if the duality were distinctly perceptible, even *that*—even this mere numerical double of his own consciousness-might be a curse too mighty to be sustained. But how, if the alien nature contradicts his own, fights with it, perplexes, and confounds it? How, again, if not one alien nature, but two, but three, but four, but five, are introduced within what once he thought the inviolable sanctuary of himself? These, however, are horrors from the kingdoms of anarchy and darkness, which, by their very intensity, challenge the sanctity of concealment, and gloomily retire from exposition. Yet it was necessary to mention them, because the first introduction to such appearances (whether causal, or merely casual) lay in the heraldic monsters, (which monsters were themselves introduced though playfully,) by the transfigured coachman of the Bath mail.

[40] "*Households*."—Roe-deer do not congregate in herds like the fallow or the red deer, but by separate families, parents, and children; which feature of approximation to the sanctity of human hearths, added to their comparatively miniature and graceful proportions, conciliate to them an interest of a peculiarly tender character, if less dignified by the grandeurs of savage and forest life.

[41] "*However visionary*."—But *are* they always visionary? The unicorn, the kraken, the sea-serpent, are all, perhaps, zoological facts. The unicorn, for instance, so far from being a lie, is rather *too* true; for, simply a *monokeras*, he is found in the Himalaya, in Africa, and elsewhere, rather too often for the peace of what in Scotland would be called the *intending* traveller. That which really *is* a lie in the account of the unicorn—viz., his legendary rivalship with the lion—which lie may God preserve, in preserving the mighty imperial shield that embalms it—cannot be more destructive to the zoological pretensions of the unicorn, than are to the same pretensions in the lion our many popular crazes about his goodness and magnanimity, or the old fancy (adopted by Spenser, and noticed by so many among our elder poets) of his graciousness to maiden innocence. The wretch is the basest and most cowardly among the forest tribes; nor has the sublime courage of the English bull-dog ever been so memorably exhibited as in his hopeless fight at Warwick with the cowardly and cruel lion called Wallace. Another of the traditional creatures, still doubtful, is

the mermaid, upon which Southey once remarked to me, that, if it had been differently named, (as, suppose, a mer-ape,) nobody would have questioned its existence any more than that of sea-cows, sea-lions, &c. The mermaid has been discredited by her human name and her legendary human habits. If she would not coquette so much with melancholy sailors, and brush her hair so assiduously upon solitary rocks, she would be carried on our books for as honest a reality, as decent a female, as many that are assessed to the poor-rates.

GOING DOWN WITH VICTORY

But the grandest chapter of our experience, within the whole mail-coach service, was on those occasions when we went down from London with the news of victory. A period of about ten years stretched from Trafalgar to Waterloo: the second and third years of which period (1806 and 1807) were comparatively sterile; but the rest, from 1805 to 1815 inclusively, furnished a long succession of victories; the least of which, in a contest of that portentous nature, had an inappreciable value of position—partly for its absolute interference with the plans of our enemy, but still more from its keeping alive in central Europe the sense of a deep-seated vulnerability in France. Even to tease the coasts of our enemy, to mortify them by continual blockades, to insult them by capturing if it were but a baubling schooner under the eyes of their arrogant armies, repeated from time to time a sullen proclamation of power lodged in a quarter to which the hopes of Christendom turned in secret. How much more loudly must this proclamation have spoken in the audacity [42] of having bearded the *élite* of their troops, and having beaten them in pitched battles! Five years of life it was worth paying down for the privilege of an outside place on a mail-coach, when carrying down the first tidings of any such event. And it is to be noted that, from our insular situation, and the multitude of our frigates disposable for the rapid transmission of intelligence, rarely did any unauthorized rumor steal away a prelibation from the aroma of the regular dispatches. The government official news was generally the first news.

[42] "*Audacity!*" Such the French accounted it; and it has struck me that Soult would not have been so popular in London, at the period of her present Majesty's coronation, or in Manchester, on occasion of his visit to that town, if they had been aware of the insolence with which he spoke of us in notes written at intervals from the field of Waterloo. As though it had been mere felony in our army to look a French on in the face, he said more than once—"Here are the English—we have them: they are caught *en flagrant délit.*" Yet no man should have known us better; no man had drunk deeper from the cup of humiliation than Soult had in the north of Portugal, during his flight from an English army, and subsequently at Albuera, in the bloodiest of recorded battles.

From eight, P. M. to fifteen or twenty minutes later, imagine the mails assembled on parade in Lombard Street, where, at that time, was seated the General Post-Office. In what exact strength we mustered I do not remember; but, from the length of each separate *attelage*, we filled the street, though a long one, and though we were drawn up in double file. On *any* night the spectacle was beautiful. The absolute perfection of all the appointments about the carriages and the harness, and the magnificence of the horses, were what might first have fixed the attention. Every carriage, on every morning in the year, was taken down to an inspector for examination— wheels, axles, linchpins, pole, glasses, &c., were all critically probed and tested. Every part of every carriage had been cleaned, every horse had been groomed, with as much rigor as if they belonged to a private gentleman; and that part of the spectacle offered itself always. But the night before us is a night of victory; and, behold! to the ordinary display, what a heart-shaking addition! horses, men, carriages all are dressed in laurels and flowers, oak leaves and ribbons. The guards, who are his majesty's servants, and the coachmen, who are within the privilege of the post-office, wear the royal liveries of course; and as it is summer (for all the *land* victories were won in summer,) they wear, on this fine evening, these liveries exposed to view, without any covering of upper coats. Such a costume, and the elaborate arrangement of the laurels in their hats, dilated their hearts, by giving to them openly an *official* connection with the great news, in which already they have the general interest of patriotism. That great national sentiment surmounts and quells all sense of ordinary distinctions. Those passengers who happen to be gentlemen are now hardly to be distinguished as such except by dress. The usual reserve of their manner in speaking to the attendants has on this night melted away. One heart, one pride, one glory, connects every man by the transcendent bond of his English blood. The spectators, who are numerous beyond precedent, express their sympathy with these fervent feelings by continual hurrahs. Every moment are shouted aloud by the post-office servants the great ancestral names of cities known to history through a thousand years,—Lincoln, Winchester, Portsmouth, Gloucester, Oxford, Bristol, Manchester, York, Newcastle, Edinburgh, Perth, Glasgow, — expressing the grandeur of the empire by the antiquity of its towns, and the grandeur of the mail establishment by the diffusive radiation of its separate missions. Every moment you hear the thunder of lids locked down upon the mail-bags. That sound to each individual mail is the signal for drawing off, which process is the finest part of the entire spectacle. Then come the horses into play,—horses! can these be horses that (unless powerfully reined in) would bound off with the action and gestures of leopards? What stir!—what sea-like ferment!— what a thundering of wheels, what a trampling of horses!—what farewell cheers—what redoubling peals of brotherly congratulation, connecting the name of the particular mail—'Liverpool for ever!'- with the name of the particular victory -'Badajoz for ever!' or 'Salamanca for ever!' The half-slumbering consciousness that, all night long and all the next day—perhaps for even a longer period many of these mails, like fire racing along a train of gunpowder, will be kindling at every instant new successions of burning joy, has an obscure effect of multiplying the victory itself, by multiplying to the imagination into infinity the stages of its progressive diffusion. A fiery arrow seems to be let loose, which from that moment is destined to travel, almost without intermission, westwards for three hundred [43] miles— northwards for six hundred; and the sympathy of our Lombard Street friends at parting is exalted a hundred fold by a sort of visionary sympathy with the approaching sympathies, yet unborn, which we are going to evoke.

[43] "*Three hundred.*" Of necessity this scale of measurement, to an American, if he happens to be a thoughtless man, must sound ludicrous. Accordingly, I remember a case in which an American writer indulges himself in the luxury of a little lying, by ascribing to an Englishman a pompous account of the Thames, constructed entirely upon American ideas of grandeur, and concluding in something like these terms:— "And, sir, arriving at London, this mighty father of rivers attains a breadth of at least two furlongs, having, in its winding course, traversed the astonishing distance of 170

miles." And this the candid American thinks it fair to contrast with the scale of the Mississippi. Now, it is hardly worth while to answer a pure falsehood gravely, else one might say that no Englishman out of Bedlam ever thought of looking in an island for the rivers of a continent; nor, consequently, could have thought of looking for the peculiar grandeur of the Thames in the length of its course, or in the extent of soil which it drains: yet, if he *had* been so absurd, the American might have recollected that a river, not to be compared with the Thames even as to volume of water—viz. the Tiber—has contrived to make itself heard of in this world for twenty-five centuries to an extent not reached, nor likely to be reached very soon, by any river, however corpulent, of his own land. The glory of the Thames is measured by the density of the population to which it ministers, by the commerce which it supports, by the grandeur of the empire in which, though far from the largest, it is the most influential stream. Upon some such scale, and not by a transfer of Columbian standards, is the course of our English mails to be valued. The American may fancy the effect of his own valuations to our English ears, by supposing the case of a Siberian glorifying his country in these terms:—"Those rascals, sir, in France and England, cannot march half a mile in any direction without finding a house where food can be had and lodging: whereas, such is the noble desolation of our magnificent county, that in many direction for a thousand miles, I will engage a dog shall not find shelter from a snow-storm, nor a wren find an apology for breakfast."

Liberated from the embarrassments of the city, and issuing into the broad uncrowded avenues of the northern suburbs, we begin to enter upon our natural pace of ten miles an hour. In the broad light of the summer evening, the sun, perhaps, only just at the point of setting, we are seen from every story of every house. Heads of every age crowd to the windows —young and old understand the language of our victorious symbols -and rolling volleys of sympathizing cheers run along behind and before our course. The beggar, rearing himself against the wall, forgets his lameness—real or assumed—thinks not of his whining trade, but stands erect, with bold exulting smiles, as we pass him. The victory has healed him, and says — Be thou whole! Women and children, from garrets alike and cellars, look down or look up with loving eyes upon our gay ribbons and our martial laurels—sometimes kiss their hands, sometimes hang out, as signals of affection, pocket handkerchiefs, aprons, dusters, anything that lies ready to their hands. On the London side of Barnet, to which we draw near within a few minutes after nine, observe that private carriage which is approaching us. The weather being so warm, the glasses are all down; and one may read, as on the stage of a theatre, everything that goes on within the carriage. It contains three ladies, one likely to be 'mama,' and two of seventeen or eighteen, who are probably her daughters. What lovely animation, what beautiful unpremeditated pantomime, explaining to us every syllable that passes, in these ingenuous girls! By the sudden start and raising of the hands, on first discovering our laurelled equipage! — by the sudden movement and appeal to the elder lady from both of them -and by the heightened color on their animated countenances, Awe can almost hear them saying — 'See, see! Look at their laurels. Oh, mama! there has been a great battle in Spain; and it has been a great victory.' In a moment we are on the point of passing them. We passengers—I on the box, and the two on the roof behind me— raise our hats, the coachman makes his professional salute with the whip; the guard even, though punctilious on the matter of his dignity as an officer under the crown, touches his hat. The ladies move to us, in return, with a winning graciousness of gesture: all smile on each side in a way that nobody could misunderstand, and that nothing short of a grand national sympathy could so instantaneously prompt. Will these ladies say that we are nothing to *them*? Oh, no; they will not say *that*. They cannot deny — they do not deny—that for this night they are our sisters: gentle or simple, scholar or illiterate servant, for twelve hours to come—we on the outside have the honor to be their brothers. Those poor women again, who stop to gaze upon us with delight at the entrance of Barnet, and seem, by their air of weariness, to be returning from labor- do you mean to say that they are washerwomen and char-women? Oh, my poor friend, you are quite mistaken; they are nothing of the kind. I assure you they stand in a higher rank; for this one night they feel themselves by birthright to be daughters of England, and answer to no humbler title.

Every joy, however, even rapturous joy —such is the sad law of earth—may carry with it grief, or fear of grief, to some. Three miles beyond Barnet, we see approaching us another private carriage, nearly repeating the circumstances of the former case. Here, also, the glasses are all down—here, also, is an elderly lady seated; but the two amiable daughters are missing; for the single young person, sitting by the lady's side, seems to be an attendant—so I judge from her dress, and her air of respectful reserve. The lady is in mourning; and her countenance expresses sorrow. At first she does not look up; so that I believe she is not aware of our approach, until she hears the measured beating of our horses' hoofs. Then she raises her eyes to settle them painfully on our triumphal equipage. Our decorations explain the case to her at once; but she beholds them with apparent anxiety, or even with terror. Some time before this, I, finding it difficult to hit a flying mark, when embarrassed by the coachman's person and reins intervening, had given to the guard a *Courier* evening paper, containing the gazette, for the next carriage that might pass. Accordingly he tossed it in so folded that the huge capitals expressing some such legend as—GLORIOUS VICTORY, might catch the eye at once. To see the paper, however, at all, interpreted as it was by our ensigns of triumph, explained everything; and, if the guard were right in thinking the lady to have received it with a gesture of horror, it could not be doubtful that she had suffered some deep personal affliction in connection with this Spanish war.

Here now was the case of one, who, having formerly suffered, might, erroneously perhaps, be distressing herself with anticipations of another similar suffering. That same night, and hardly three hours later, occurred the reverse case. A poor woman, who too probably would find herself, in a day or two, to have suffered the heaviest of afflictions by the battle, blindly allowed herself to express an exultation so unmeasured in the news, and its details, as gave to her the appearance which amongst Celtic Highlanders is called *fey*. This was at some little town, I forget what, where we happened to change horses near midnight. Some fair or wake had kept the people up out of their beds. We saw many lights moving about as we drew near; and perhaps the most impressive scene on our route was our reception at this place. The flashing of torches and the beautiful radiance of blue lights (technically Bengal lights) upon the heads of our horses: the fine effect of such a showery and ghostly illumination falling upon flowers and glittering laurels, whilst all around the massy darkness seemed to invest us with walls of impenetrable blackness, together with the prodigious enthusiasm of the people, composed a picture at once scenical and affecting. As we staid for three or four minutes, I alighted. And immediately from a dismantled stall in the street, where perhaps she had been presiding at some part of the evening, advanced eagerly a middle-aged woman. The sight of my newspaper it was that had drawn her attention upon myself. The victory which we were carrying down to the provinces on this occasion was the imperfect one of Talavera. I told her the main outline of the battle. But her agitation, though not the agitation of fear, but of exultation rather, and enthusiasm, had been so conspicuous when listening, and when first applying for information, that I could not but ask her if she had not some relation in the Peninsular army. Oh! yes: her only son was there. In what regiment? He was a trooper in the 03d Dragoons. My heart sank within me as she made that answer. This sublime regiment, which an Englishman should never mention without raising his hat to their memory, had made the most memorable and effective charge recorded in military annals. They leaped their horses—*over* a trench where they could, *into* it, and with the result of death or mutilation when they could *not*. What proportion cleared the trench is nowhere stated. Those who *did*, closed up and went down upon the enemy with such divinity of fervor— (I use the word *divinity* by design: the inspiration of God must have prompted this movement to those whom even then he was calling to his presence)—that two results followed. As regarded the enemy, this 2d Dragoons, not, I believe, originally three hundred and fifty strong, paralyzed a French column, six thousand strong, then ascending the hill, and fixed the gaze of the whole French army. As regarded themselves, the 23d were supposed at first to have been all but annihilated; but eventually, I believe, not so many as one in four survived. And this, then, was the regiment—a regiment already for some hours known to myself and all London, as stretched, by a large majority, upon one bloody aceldama—in which the young trooper served whose mother was now talking with myself in a spirit of such hopeful enthusiasm. Did I tell her the truth? Had I the heart to break up her dreams? No. I said to myself, to-morrow, or the next day, she will hear the worst. For this night, wherefore should she not sleep in peace? After to-morrow, the chances are too many that peace will forsake her pillow. This brief respite, let her owe this to *my* gift and *my* forbearance. But, if I. told her not of the bloody price that had been paid, there was no reason for suppressing the contributions from her son's regiment to the service and glory of the day. For the very few words that I had time for speaking, I governed myself accordingly. I showed her not the funeral banners under which the noble regiment was sleeping. I lifted not the overshadowing laurels from the bloody trench in which horse and rider lay mangled together. But I told her how these dear children of England, privates and officers, had leaped their horses over all obstacles as gaily as hunters to the morning's chase. I told her how they rode their horses into the mists of death, (saying to myself, but not saying to *her*,) and laid down their young lives for thee, O mother England! as willingly—poured out their noble blood as cheerfully—as ever, after a long day's sport, when infants, they had rested their wearied heads upon their mother's knees, or had sunk to sleep in her arms. It is singular that she seemed to have no fears, even after this knowledge that the 23d Dragoons had been conspicuously engaged, for her son's safety: but so much was she enraptured by the knowledge that his regiment, and therefore *he*, had rendered eminent service in the trying conflict—a service which had actually made them the foremost topic of conversation in London—that in the mere simplicity of her fervent nature, she threw her arms round my neck, and, poor woman, kissed me.

THE VISION OF SUDDEN DEATH

What is to be thought of sudden death? It is remarkable that, in different conditions of society it has been variously regarded as the consummation of an earthly career most fervently to be desired, and, on the other hand, as that consummation which is most of all to be deprecated. Caesar the Dictator, at his last dinner party, (*cœna*,) and the very evening before his assassination, being questioned as to the mode of death which, in *his* opinion, might seem the most eligible, replied -' That which should be most sudden.' On the other hand, the divine Litany of our English Church, when breathing forth supplications, as if in some representative character for the whole human race prostrate before God, places such a death in the very van of horrors. 'From lightning and tempest; from plague, pestilence, and famine; from battle and murder, and from sudden death,— *Good Lord, deliver us*.' Sudden death is here made to crown the climax in a grand ascent of calamities; it is the last of curses; and yet, by the noblest of Romans, it was treated as the first of blessings.) In that difference, most readers will see little more than the difference between Christianity and Paganism. But there I hesitate. The Christian church may be right in its estimate of sudden death; and it is a natural feeling, though after all it may also be an infirm one, to wish for a quiet dismissal from life—as that which seems most reconcilable with meditation, with penitential retrospects, and with the humilities of farewell prayer. There does not, however, occur to me any. direct scriptural warrant for this earnest petition of the English Litany. It seems rather a petition indulged to human infirmity, than exacted from human piety. And, however that may be, two remarks suggest themselves as prudent restraints upon a doctrine, which else *may* wander, and *has* wandered, into an uncharitable superstition. The first is this: that many people are likely to exaggerate the horror of a sudden death, (I mean the *objective* horror to him who contemplates such a death, not the *subjective* horror to him who suffers it,) from the false disposition to lay a stress upon words or acts, simply because by an accident they have become *final* words or acts. If a man dies, for instance, by some sudden death when he happens to be intoxicated, such a death is falsely regarded with peculiar horror; as though the intoxication were suddenly exalted into a blasphemy. But that is unphilosophic. The man was, or he was not, *habitually* a drunkard. If not, if his intoxication were a solitary accident, there can be no reason at all for allowing special emphasis to this act, simply because through misfortune it became his final act. Nor, on the other hand, if it were no accident, but one of his habitual transgressions, will it be the more habitual or the more a transgression, because some sudden calamity, surprising him, has caused this habitual transgression to be also a final one? Could the man have had any reason even dimly to foresee his own sudden death, there would have been a new feature in his act of intemperance -a feature of presumption and irreverence, as in one that by possibility felt himself drawing near to the presence of God. But this is no part of the case supposed. And the only new element in the man's act is not any element of extra immorality, but simply of extra misfortune.

The other remark has reference to the meaning of the word *sudden*. And it is a strong illustration of the duty which for ever calls us to the stern valuation of words — that very possibly Caesar and the Christian church do not differ in the way supposed; that is, do not differ by any difference of doctrine as between Pagan and Christian views of the moral temper appropriate to death, but that they are contemplating different cases. Both contemplate a violent death, a βιαθανατος;—death that is βιαιος: but the difference is — that the Roman by the word 'sudden' means an *unlingering* death: whereas the Christian Litany by 'sudden' means a death *without warning*, consequently without any available summons to religious preparation. The poor mutineer, who kneels down to gather into his heart the bullets from twelve firelocks of his pitying comrades, dies by a most sudden death in Caesar's sense: one shock, one mighty spasm, one (possibly *not* one) groan, and all is over. But, in the sense of the Litany, his death is far from sudden; his offence, originally, his imprisonment, his trial, the interval between his sentence and its execution, having all furnished him with separate warnings of his fate - having all summoned him to meet it with solemn preparation.

Meantime, whatever may be thought of a sudden death as a mere variety in the modes of dying, where death in some shape is inevitable—a question which, equally in the Roman and the Christian sense, will be variously answered according to each man's variety of temperament—certainly, upon one aspect of sudden death there can be no opening for doubt, that of all agonies incident to man it is the most frightful, that of all martyrdoms it is the most freezing to human sensibilities—namely, where it surprises a man under circumstances which offer (or which seem to offer) some hurried and inappreciable chance of evading it. Any effort, by which such an evasion can be accomplished, must be as sudden as the danger which it affronts. Even *that*, even the sickening necessity for hurrying in extremity where all hurry seems destined to be vain, self-baffled, and where the dreadful knell of *too late* is already sounding in the ears by anticipation—even that anguish is liable to a hideous exasperation in one particular case, namely, where the agonizing appeal is made not exclusively to the instinct of self-preservation, but to the conscience, on behalf of another life besides your own, accidentally cast upon *your* protection. To fail, to collapse in a service merely your own, might seem comparatively venial; though, in fact, it is far from venial: But to fail in a case where Providence has suddenly thrown into your hands the final interests of another—of a fellow-creature shuddering between the gates of life and death; this, to a man of apprehensive conscience, would mingle the misery of an atrocious criminality with the misery of a bloody calamity. The man is called upon, too probably, to die; but to die at the very moment when, by any momentary collapse, he is self-denounced as a murderer. He had but the twinkling of an eye for his effort, and that effort might, at the best, have been unavailing; but from this shadow of a chance, small or great, how if he has recoiled by a treasonable *lâcheté?* The effort *might* have been without hope; but to have risen to the level of that effort, would have rescued him, though not from dying, yet from dying as a traitor to his duties.

The situation here contemplated exposes a dreadful ulcer, lurking far down in the depths of human nature. It is not that men generally are summoned to face such awful trials. But potentially, and in shadowy outline, such a trial is moving subterranously in perhaps all men's natures—muttering under ground in one world, to be realized perhaps in some other. Upon the secret mirror of our dreams such a trial is darkly projected at intervals, perhaps, to every one of us. That dream, so familiar to childhood, of meeting a lion, and, from languishing prostration in hope and vital energy, that constant sequel of lying down before him, publishes the secret frailty of human nature - reveals its deep-seated Pariah falsehood to itself — records its abysmal treachery. Perhaps not one of us escapes that dream; perhaps, as by some sorrowful doom of man, that dream repeats for every one of us, through every generation, the original temptation in Eden. Every one of us, in this dream, has a bait offered to the infirm places of his own individual will; once again a snare is made ready for leading him into captivity to a luxury of ruin; again, as in aboriginal Paradise, the man falls from innocence; once again, by infinite iteration, the ancient Earth groans to God, through her secret caves, over the weakness of her child;' Nature, from her seat, sighing through all her works,' again' gives signs of woe that all is lost;' and again the counter sigh is repeated to the sorrowing heavens of the endless rebellion against God. Many people think that one man, the patriarch of our race, could not in his single person execute this rebellion for all his race. Perhaps they are wrong. But, even if not, perhaps in the world of dreams every one of us ratifies for himself the original act. Our English right of 'Confirmation,' by which, in years of awakened reason, we take upon us the engagements contracted for us in our slumbering infancy,- how sublime a rite is that! The little postern gate, through which the baby in its cradle had been silently placed for a time within the glory of God's countenance, suddenly rises to the clouds as a triumphal arch, through which, with banners displayed and martial pomps, we make our second entry as crusading soldiers militant for God, by personal choice and by sacramental oath. Each man says in effect—' Lo! I rebaptize myself; and that which once was sworn on my behalf, now I swear for myself.' Even so in dreams, perhaps, under some secret conflict of the midnight sleeper, lighted up to the consciousness at the time, but darkened to the memory as soon as all is finished, each several child of our mysterious race completes for himself the aboriginal fall.

As I drew near to the Manchester post-office, I found that it was considerably past midnight; but to my great relief, as it was important for me to be in Westmoreland by the morning, I saw by the huge saucer eyes of the. mail, blazing through the gloom of overhanging houses, that my chance was not yet lost. Past the time it was; but by some luck, very unusual in my experience, the mail was not even yet ready to start. I ascended to my seat on the box, where my cloak was still lying as it had lain at the Bridgewater Arms. I had left it there in imitation of a nautical discoverer, who leaves a bit of bunting on the shore of his discovery, by way of warning off the ground the whole human race, and signalizing to the Christian and the heathen worlds, with his best compliments, that he has planted his throne for ever upon that virgin soil: henceforward claiming the *jus dominii* to, the top of the atmosphere above it, and also the right of driving shafts to the centre of the earth below it; so that all people found after this warning, either aloft in the atmosphere, or in the shafts, or squatting on the soil, will be treated as trespassers— that is, decapitated by their very faithful and obedient servant, the owner of the said bunting. Possibly my cloak might not have been respected, and the *jus gentium* might have been cruelly violated in my person — for, in the dark, people commit deeds of darkness, gas being a great ally of morality- but it so happened that, on this night, there was no other outside passenger; and the crime, which else was but too probable, missed fire for want of a criminal. By the way, I may as well mention at this point, since a circumstantial accuracy is essential to the effect of my narrative, that there was no other person of any description whatever about the mail—the guard, the coachman, and myself being allowed for—except only one—a horrid creature of the class known to the world as insiders, but whom young Oxford called sometimes 'Trojans,' in opposition to our Grecian selves, and sometimes 'vermin.' A Turkish Effendi, who piques himself on good breeding, will never mention by name a pig. Yet it is but too often that he has reason to mention this animal; since constantly, in the streets of Stamboul, he has his trousers deranged or polluted by this vile creature running between his legs. But under any excess of hurry he is always careful, out of respect to the company he is dining with, to suppress the odious name, and to call the wretch 'that other creature,' as though all animal life beside formed one group, and this odious beast (to whom, as Chrysippus observed, salt serves as an apology for a soul) formed another and alien group on the outside of creation. Now I, who am an English Effendi, that think myself to understand good-breeding as well as any son of Othman, beg my reader's pardon for having mentioned an insider by his gross natural name. I shall do so no more: and, if I should have occasion to glance at so painful a subject, I shall always call him 'that other creature.' Let us hope, however, that no such distressing occasion will arise. But, by the way, an occasion arises at this moment; for the reader will be sure to ask, when we come to the story,' Was this other creature present?'

He was not; or more correctly, perhaps, it was not. We dropped the creature—or the creature, by natural imbecility dropped itself- within the first ten miles from Manchester. In the latter case, I wish to make a philosophic remark of a moral tendency. When I die, or when the reader dies, and by repute suppose of fever, it will never be known whether we died in reality of the fever or of the doctor. But this other creature, in the case of dropping out of the coach, will enjoy a coroner's inquest; consequently he will enjoy an epitaph. For I insist upon it, that the verdict of a coroner's jury makes the best of epitaphs. It is brief, so that the public all find time to read; it is pithy, so that the surviving friends (if any can survive such a loss) remember it without fatigue; it is upon oath, so that rascals and Dr. Johnsons cannot pick holes in it. 'Died through the visitation of intense stupidity, by impinging on a moonlight night against the off hind wheel of the Glasgow mail! Deodand upon the said wheel—two-pence.' What a simple lapidary inscription! Nobody much in the wrong but an off-wheel; and with few acquaintances; and if it were but rendered into choice Latin, though there would be a little bother in finding a Ciceronian word for 'off-wheel,' Marcellus himself, that great master of sepulchral eloquence, could not show a better. Why I call this little remark *moral*, is, from the compensation it points out. Here, by the supposition, is that other creature on the one side, the beast of the world; and he (or it) gets an epitaph. You and I, on the contrary, the pride of our friends, get none.

But why linger on the subject of vermin? Having mounted the box, I took a small quantity of laudanum, having already travelled two hundred and fifty miles—viz., from a point seventy miles beyond London, upon a simple breakfast. In the taking of laudanum there was nothing extraordinary. But by accident it drew upon me the special attention of my assessor on the box, the coachman. And in *that* there was nothing extraordinary. But by accident, and with great delight, it drew my attention to the fact that this coachman was a monster in point of size, and that he had but one eye. In fact he had been foretold by Virgil as

"Monstrum horrendum, informe, ingens cui lumen ademptum."

He answered in every point—a monster he was— dreadful, shapeless, huge, who had lost an eye. But why should *that* delight me? Had he been one of the Calendars in the Arabian Nights, and had paid down his eye as the price of his criminal curiosity, what right had *I* to exult in his misfortune? I did *not* exult: I delighted in no man's punishment, though it were even merited. But these personal distinctions identified in an instant an old friend of mine, whom I had known in the south for some years as the most masterly of mail-coachmen. He was the man in all Europe that could best have undertaken to drive six-in-hand full gallop over *Al Sirat*—that famous bridge of Mahomet across the bottomless gulf, backing himself against the Prophet and twenty such fellows. I used to call him *Cyclops Mastigophorus*, Cyclops the whip-bearer, until I observed that his skill made whips useless, except to fetch off an impertinent fly from a leader's head; upon which I changed his Grecian name to Cyclops *diphrélates* (Cyclops the charioteer.) I, and others known to me, studied under him the diphrelatic art. Excuse, reader, a word too elegant to be pedantic. And also take this remark from me, as a *gage d'amitié*—that no word ever was or *can* be pedantic which, by supporting a distinction, supports the accuracy of logic; or which fills up a chasm for the understanding. As a pupil, though I paid extra fees, I cannot say that I stood high in his esteem. It showed his dogged honesty, (though, observe, not his discernment,) that he could not see my merits. Perhaps we ought to excuse his absurdity in this particular by remembering his want of an eye. *That* made him blind to my merits. Irritating as this blindness was, (surely it could not be envy!) he always courted my conversation, in which art I certainly had the whip-hand of him. On this occasion, great joy was at our meeting. But what was Cyclops doing here? Had the medical men recommended northern air, or how? I collected, from such explanations as he volunteered, that he had an interest at stake in a suit-at-law pending at Lancaster; so that probably he had got himself transferred to this station, for the purpose of connecting with his professional pursuits an instant readiness for the calls of his law-suit.

Meantime, what are we stopping for? Surely, we've been waiting long enough. Oh, this procrastinating mail, and oh this procrastinating post-office! Can't they take a lesson upon that subject from *me*? Some people have called *me* procrastinating. Now you are witness, reader, that I was in time for *them*. But can *they* lay their hands on their hearts, and say that they were in time for me? I, during my life, have often had to wait for the post-office: the post-office never waited a minute for me. What are they about? The guard tells me that there is a large extra accumulation of foreign mails this night, owing to irregularities caused by war and by the packet service, when as yet nothing is done by steam. For an *extra* hour, it seems, the post-office has been engaged in threshing out the pure wheaten correspondence of Glasgow, and winnowing it from the chaff of all baser intermediate towns. We can hear the flails going at this moment. But at last all is finished. Sound your horn, guard. Manchester, good bye; we've lost an hour by your criminal conduct at the post-office: which, however, though I do not mean to part with a serviceable ground of complaint, and one which really *is* such for the horses, to me secretly is an advantage, since it compels us to recover this last hour amongst the next eight or nine. Off we are at last, and at eleven miles an hour; and at first I detect no changes in the energy or in the skill of Cyclops.

From Manchester to Kendal, which virtually (though not in law) is the capital of Westmoreland, were at this time seven stages of eleven miles each. The first five of these, dated from Manchester, terminated in Lancaster, which was therefore fifty-five miles north of Manchester, and the same distance exactly from Liverpool. The first three terminated in Preston, (called, by way of distinction from other towns of that name, proud Preston,) at which place it was that the separate roads from Liverpool and from Manchester to the north became confluent. Within these first three stages lay the foundation, the progress, and termination of our night's adventure. During the first stage, I found out that Cyclops was mortal: he was liable to the shocking affection of sleep—a thing which I had never previously suspected. If a man is addicted to the vicious habit of sleeping, all the skill in aurigation of Apollo himself, with the horses of Aurora to execute the motions of his will, avail him nothing.' Oh, Cyclops!' I exclaimed more than once,' Cyclops, my friend; thou art mortal. Thou snorest.' Through this first eleven miles, however, he betrayed his infirmity—which I grieve to say he shared with the whole Pagan Pantheon-only by short stretches. On waking up, he made an apology for himself, which, instead of mending the matter, laid an ominous foundation for coming disasters. The summer assizes were now proceeding at Lancaster: in consequence of which, for three nights and three days, he had not lain down in a bed. During the day, he was waiting for his uncertain summons as a witness on the trial in which he was interested; or he was drinking with the other witnesses, under the vigilant surveillance of the attorneys. During the night, or that part of it when the least temptations existed to conviviality, he was driving. Throughout the second stage he grew more and more drowsy. In the second mile of the third stage, he surrendered himself finally and without a struggle to his perilous temptation. All his past resistance had but deepened the weight of this final oppression. Seven atmospheres of sleep seemed resting upon him; and to consummate the case, our worthy guard, after singing, 'Love amongst the Roses,' for the fiftieth or sixtieth time, without any invitation from Cyclops or myself, and without applause for his poor labors, had moodily resigned himself to slumber—not so deep doubtless as the coachman's, but deep enough for mischief; and having, probably, no similar excuse. And thus at last, about ten miles from Preston, I found myself left in charge of his Majesty's London and Glasgow mail, then running about eleven miles an hour.

What made this negligence less criminal than else it must have been thought, was the condition of the roads at night during the assizes. At that time all the law business of populous Liverpool, and of populous Manchester, with its vast cincture of populous rural districts, was called up by ancient usage to the tribunal of Lilliputian Lancaster. To break up this old traditional usage required a conflict with powerful established interests, a large system of new arrangements, and a new parliamentary statute. As things were at present, twice in the year so vast a body of business rolled northwards, from the southern quarter of the county, that a fortnight at least occupied the severe exertions of two judges for its dispatch. The consequence of this was—that every horse available for such a service, along the whole line of road, was exhausted in carrying down the multitudes of people who were parties to the different suits. By sunset, therefore, it usually happened that, through utter exhaustion amongst men and horses, the roads were all silent. Except exhaustion in the vast adjacent county of York from a contested election, nothing like it was ordinarily witnessed in England.

On this occasion, the usual silence and solitude prevailed along the road. Not a hoof nor a wheel was to be heard. And to strengthen this false luxurious confidence in the noiseless roads, it happened also that the night was one of peculiar solemnity and peace. I myself, though slightly alive to the possibilities of peril, had so far yielded to the influence of the mighty calm as to sink into a profound reverie. The month was August, in which lay my own birth-day; a festival to every thoughtful man suggesting solemn and often. sigh-born thoughts [44]. The county was my own native county- upon which, in its southern section, more than upon any equal area known to man past or present, had descended the original curse of labor in its heaviest form, not mastering the bodies of men only as of slaves, or criminals in mines, but working through the fiery will. Upon no equal space of earth, was, or ever had been, the same energy of human power put forth daily. At this particular season also of the assizes, that dreadful hurricane of flight and pursuit, as it might have seemed to a stranger, that swept to and from Lancaster all day long, hunting the county up and down, and regularly subsiding about sunset, united with the permanent distinction of Lancashire as the very metropolis and citadel of labor, to point the thoughts pathetically upon that counter vision of rest, of saintly repose from strife and sorrow, towards which, as to their secret haven, the profounder aspirations of man's heart are continually travelling. Obliquely we were nearing the sea upon our left, which also must, under the present circumstances, be repeating the general state of halcyon repose. The sea, the atmosphere, the light, bore an orchestral part in this universal lull. Moonlight, in the first timid tremblings of the dawn, were now blending: and the blendings were brought into a still more exquisite state of unity, by a slight silvery mist, motionless and dreamy, that covered the woods and fields, but with a veil of equable transparency. Except the feet of our own horses, which, running on a sandy margin of the road, made little disturbance, there was no sound abroad. In the clouds, and on the earth, prevailed the same majestic peace; and in spite of all that the villain of a

94

school. master has done for the ruin of our sublimer thoughts, which are the thoughts of our infancy, we still believe in no such nonsense as a limited atmosphere. Whatever we may swear with our false feigning lips, in our faithful hearts we still believe, and must for ever believe, in fields of air traversing the total gulf between earth and the central heavens. Still, in the confidence of children that tread without fear every chamber in their father's house, and to whom no door is closed, we, in that Sabbatic vision which sometimes is revealed for an hour upon nights like this, ascend with easy steps from the sorrow-stricken fields of earth, upwards to the sandals of God.

[44] "Sigh-born:" I owe the suggestion of this world to an obscure remembrance of a beautiful phrase in Giraldus Cambrensis, viz., *suspiriosae cognitationes.*

Suddenly from thoughts like these, I was awakened to a sullen sound, as of some motion on the distant road. It stole upon the air for a moment; I listened in awe; but then it died away. Once roused, however, I could not but observe with alarm the quickened motion of our horses. Ten years' experience had made my eye learned in the valuing of motion; and I saw that we were now running thirteen miles an hour. I pretend to no presence of mind. On the contrary, my fear is, that I am miserably and shamefully deficient in that quality as regards *action*. The palsy of doubt and distraction hangs like some guilty weight of dark unfathomed remembrances upon nay energies, when the signal is flying for action. But, on the other hand, this accursed gift I have, as regards. thought, that in the first step towards the possibility of a misfortune, I see its total evolution: in the radix I see too certainly and too instantly its entire expansion; in the first syllable of the dreadful sentence, I read already the last. It was not that I feared for ourselves. What could injure *us*? Our bulk and impetus charmed us against peril in any collision. And I had rode through too many hundreds of perils that were frightful to approach, that were matter of laughter as we looked back upon them, for any anxiety to rest upon *our* interests. The mail was not built, I felt assured, nor bespoke, that could betray *me* who trusted to its protection. But any carriage that we could meet would be frail and light in comparison of ourselves. And I remarked this ominous accident of our situation. We were on the wrong side of the road. But then the other party, if other there was, might also be on the wrong side; and two wrongs might make a right. *That* was not likely. The same motive which had drawn us to the right-hand side of the road, viz., the soft beaten sand, as contrasted with the paved centre, would prove attractive to others. Our lamps, still lighted, would give the impression of vigilance on our part. And every creature that met us, would rely upon *us* for quartering [45]. All this, and if the separate links of the anticipation had been a thousand times more, I saw — not discursively or by effort- but as by one flash of horrid intuition.

[45] "Quartering"—this is the technical word; and, I presume, derived from the French *cartayer*, to evade a rut or any obstacle.

Under this steady though rapid anticipation of the evil which *might* be gathering ahead, ah, reader! what a sullen mystery of fear, what a sigh of woe, seemed to steal upon the air, as again the far-off sound of a wheel was heard! A whisper it was—a whisper from, perhaps, four miles off — secretly announcing a ruin that, being foreseen, was not the less inevitable. What could be done—who was it that could do it—to check the storm-flight of these maniacal horses? What! could I not seize the reins from the grasp of the slumbering coachman? You, reader, think that it would have been in *your* power to do so. And I quarrel not with your estimate of yourself. But, from the way in which the coachman's hand was viced between his upper and lower thigh, this was impossible. The guard subsequently found it impossible, after this danger had passed. Not the grasp only, but also the position of this Polyphemus, made the attempt impossible. You still think otherwise. See, then, that bronze equestrian statue. The cruel rider has kept the bit in his horse's mouth for two centuries. Unbridle him, for a minute, if you please, and wash his mouth with water. Or stay, reader, unhorse me that marble emperor: knock me those marble feet from those marble stirrups of Charlemagne.

The sounds ahead strengthened, and were now too clearly the sounds of wheels. Who and what could it be? Was it industry in a taxed cart? Was it youthful gaiety in a gig? Whoever it was, something must be attempted to warn them. Upon the other party rests the active responsibility, but upon us —and, woe is me! that us was my single self —rest the responsibility of warning. Yet, how should this be accomplished? Might I not seize the guard's horn? Already, on the first thought, I was making my way over the roof to the guard's seat. But this, from the foreign mail's being piled upon the roof, was a difficult, and even dangerous attempt, to one cramped by nearly three hundred miles of outside travelling. And, fortunately, before I had lost much time in the attempt, our frantic horses swept round an angle of the road, which opened upon us the stage where the collision must be accomplished, the parties that seemed summoned to the trial, and the impossibility of saving them by any communication with the guard.

Before us lay an avenue, straight as an arrow, six hundred yards, perhaps, in length; and the umbrageous trees, which rose in a regular line from either side, meeting high overhead, gave to it the character of a cathedral aisle. These trees lent a deeper solemnity to the early light; but there was still light enough to perceive, at the further end of this gothic aisle, a light, reedy gig, in which were seated a young man, and, by his side, a young lady. Ah, young sir! what are you about? If it is necessary that you should whisper your communications to this young lady- though really I see nobody at this hour, and on this solitary road, likely to overhear your conversation— is it, therefore, necessary that you should carry your lips forward to hers? The little carriage is creeping on at one mile an hour; and the parties within it, being thus tenderly engaged, are naturally bending down their heads. Between them and eternity, to all human calculation, there is but a minute and a half. What is it that I shall do? Strange it is, and to a mere auditor of the tale, might seem laughable, that I should need a suggestion from the *Iliad* to prompt the sole recourse that remained. But so it was. Suddenly I remembered the shout of Achilles, and its effect. But could I pretend to shout like the son of Peleus, aided by Pallas? No, certainly: but then I needed not the shout that should alarm all Asia militant; a shout would suffice, such as should carry terror into the hearts of two thoughtless young people, and one gig horse. I shouted—and the young man heard me not. A second time I shouted—and now he heard me, for now he raised his head.

Here, then, all had been done that, by me, *could* be done: more on *my* part was not possible. Mine had been the first step: the second was for the young man: the third was for God. If, said I, the stranger is a brave man, and if, indeed, he loves the young girl at his side—or, loving her not, if he feels the obligation pressing upon every man worthy to be called a man, of doing his utmost for a woman confided to his protection — he will at least make some effort to save her. If *that* fails, he will not perish the more, or by a death more cruel, for having made it; and he will die as a brave man should, with his face to the danger, and with his arm about the woman that he sought in vain to save. But if he makes no effort, shrinking, without a struggle, from his duty, he himself will not the less certainly perish for this baseness of poltroonery. He will die no less: and why not? Wherefore should we grieve that there is one craven less in the world? No; let him perish, without a pitying thought of ours wasted upon him; and, in that. case, all our grief will be reserved for the fate of the helpless girl, who now, upon the least shadow of failure in *him*, must, by the fiercest of translations must, without time for a prayer—must, within seventy seconds, stand before the judgment-seat of God.

But craven he was not: sudden had been the call upon him, and sudden was his answer to the call. He saw, he heard, he comprehended, the ruin that was coming down: already its gloomy shadow darkened above him; and already he was measuring his strength to deal with it. Ah! what a vulgar thing does courage seem, when we see nations buying it and selling it for a shilling a day: ah! what a sublime thing does courage seem, when some fearful crisis on the great deeps of life carries a man, as if running before a hurricane, up to the giddy crest of some mountainous wave, from which accordingly as he chooses his course, he describes two courses, and a voice says to him audibly,' This way lies hope; take the other way and mourn for ever.' Yet, even then, amidst the raving of the seas and the frenzy of the danger, the man is able to confront his situation -is able to retire for a moment into solitude with God, and to seek all his counsel from *him*! For seven seconds, it might be, of his seventy, the stranger settled his countenance steadfastly upon us, as if to search and value every element in the conflict before him. For five seconds more he sate immovably, like one that mused on some great purpose. For five he sate with eyes upraised, like one that prayed in sorrow, under some extremity of doubt, for wisdom to guide him towards the better choice. Then suddenly he rose; stood upright; and, by a sudden strain upon the reins, raising his horse's forefeet from the ground, he slewed him round on the pivot of his hind legs, so as to plant the little equipage in a position nearly at right angles to ours. Thus far his condition was not improved; except as a first step had been taken towards the possibility of a second. If no more were done, nothing was done; for the little carriage still occupied the very centre of our path, though in an altered direction. Yet even now it may not be too late: fifteen of the twenty seconds may still be unexhausted; and one almighty bound forward may avail to clear the ground. Hurry then, hurry! for the flying moments—*they* hurry! Oh hurry, hurry, my brave young man! for the cruel hoofs of our horses—*they* also hurry! Fast are the flying moments, faster are the hoofs of our horses. Fear not for him, if human energy can suffice: faithful was he that drove, to his terrific duty; faithful was the horse to *his* command. One blow, one impulse given with voice and hand by the stranger, one rush from the horse, one bound as if in the act of rising to a fence, landed the docile creature's forefeet upon the crown or arching centre of the road. The larger half of the little equipage had then cleared our over-towering shadow: *that* was evident even to my own agitated sight. But it mattered little that one wreck should float off in safety, if upon the wreck that perished were embarked the human freightage. The rear part of the carriage—was *that* certainly beyond the line of absolute ruin? What power could answer the question? Glance of eye, thought of man, wing of angel, which of these had speed enough to sweep between the question and the answer, and. divide the one from the other? Light does not tread upon the steps of light more indivisibly, than did our all-conquering arrival upon the escaping efforts of the gig. *That* must the young man have felt too plainly. His back was now turned to us; not by sight could he any longer communicate with the peril; but by the dreadful rattle of our harness, too truly had his ear been instructed—that all was finished as regarded any further effort of *his*. Already in resignation he had rested from his struggle; and perhaps, in his heart he was whispering -' Father, which art above, do thou finish in heaven what I on earth have attempted.' We ran past them faster than ever mill-race in our inexorable flight. Oh, raving of hurricanes that must have sounded in their young ears at the moment of our transit! Either with the swingle-bar, or with the haunch of our near leader, we had struck the off-wheel of the little gig, which stood rather obliquely and not quite so far advanced as to be accurately parallel with the near wheel. The blow, from the fury of our passage, resounded terrifically. I rose in horror, to look upon the ruins we might have caused. From my elevated station I looked down, and looked back upon the scene, which in a moment told its tale, and wrote all its records on my heart for ever.

The horse was planted immovably, with his fore-feet upon the paved crest of the central road. He of the whole party was alone untouched by the passion of death. The little cany carriage- partly perhaps from the dreadful torsion of the wheels in its recent movement, partly from the thundering blow we had given to it —as if it sympathized with human horror, was all alive with tremblings and shiverings. The young man sat like a rock. He stirred not at all. But *his* was the steadiness of agitation frozen into rest by horror. As yet he dared not to look round; for he knew that, if anything remained to do, by him it could no longer be done. And as yet he knew not for certain if their safety were accomplished. But the lady—

But the lady—! Oh heavens! will that spectacle ever depart from my dreams, as she rose and sank upon her seat, sank and rose, threw up her arms wildly to heaven, clutched at some visionary object in the air, fainting, praying, raving, despairing! Figure to yourself, reader, the elements of the case; suffer me to recall before your mind the circumstances of the unparalleled situation. From the silence and deep peace of this saintly summer night—from the pathetic blending of this sweet moonlight, dawnlight, dreamlight — from the manly tenderness of this flattering, whispering, murmuring love— suddenly as from the woods and fields—suddenly as from the chambers of the air opening in revelation—suddenly as from the ground yawning at her feet, leaped upon her, with the flashing of cataracts, Death the crowned phantom, with all the equipage of his terrors, and the tiger roar of his voice.

The moments were numbered. In the twinkling of an eye our flying horses had carried us to the termination of the umbrageous aisle; at right angles we wheeled into our former direction; the turn of the road carried the scene out of my eyes in an instant, and swept it into my dreams for ever.

DREAM-FUGUE

On the above theme of sudden death

'Whence the sound
Of instruments, that made melodious chime,
Was heard, of harp and organ; and who mov'd
Their stops and chords, was seen; his volant touch
Instinct through all proportions, low and high,
Fled and pursued transverse the resonant fugue.'
Par. Lost, B.xi.
Tumultuosissimamente

Passion of Sudden Death! that once in youth I read and interpreted by the shadows of thy averted [46] I signs! Rapture of panic taking the shape which amongst tombs in churches I have seen, of woman bursting her sepulchral bonds—of woman's Ionic form bending forward from the ruins of her grave with arching foot, with eyes upraised, with clasped adoring hands—waiting, watching, trembling, praying, for the trumpet's call to rise from dust for ever!—Ah, vision too fearful of shuddering humanity on the brink of abysses! vision that didst start back—that didst reel away—like a shrivelling scroll from before the wrath of fire racing on the wings of the wind! Epilepsy so brief of horror—wherefore is it that thou canst not die? Passing so suddenly into darkness, wherefore is it that still thou sheddest thy sad funeral blights upon the gorgeous mosaics of dreams? Fragment of music too stern, heard once and heard no more, what aileth thee that thy deep rolling chords come up at intervals through all the worlds of sleep, and after thirty years have lost no element of horror?

[46] "*Averted signs.*"—I read the course and changed of the lady's agony in the succession of her involuntary gestures; but let it be remembered that I read all this from the rear, never once catching the lady's full face, and even her profile imperfectly.

1

Lo, it is summer, almighty summer! The everlasting gates of life and summer are thrown open wide; and on the ocean, tranquil and verdant as a savanna, the unknown lady from the dreadful vision and I myself are floating: she upon a fairy pinnace, and I upon an English three-decker. But both of us are wooing gales of festal happiness within the domain of our common country—within that ancient watery park within that pathless chase where England takes her pleasure as a huntress through winter and summer, and which stretches from the rising to the setting sun. Ah! what a wilderness of floral beauty was hidden, or was suddenly revealed, upon the tropic islands, through which the pinnace moved. And upon her deck what a bevy of human flowers - young women how lovely, young men how noble, that were dancing together, and slowly drifting towards *us* amidst music and incense, amidst blossoms from forests and gorgeous corymbi from vintages, amidst natural carolling and the echoes of sweet girlish laughter. Slowly the pinnace nears us, gaily she hails us, and slowly she disappears beneath the shadow of our mighty bows. But then, as at some signal from heaven, the music and the carols, and the sweet echoing of girlish laughter— all are hushed. What evil has smitten the pinnace, meeting or overtaken her? Did ruin to our friends couch within our own dreadful shadow-? Was our shadow the shadow of death? I looked over the bow for an answer; and, behold! the pinnace was dismantled; the revel and the revellers were found no more; the glory of the vintage was dust; and the forest was left without a witness to its beauty upon the seas.' But where,' and I turned to our own crew -' Where are the lovely women that danced beneath the awning of flowers and clustering corymbi? Whither have fled the noble young men that danced with *them*?' Answer there was none. But suddenly the man at the mast-head, whose countenance darkened with alarm, cried out -' Sail on the weather beam! Down she comes upon us: in seventy seconds she will founder.'

2

I looked to the weather side, and the summer had departed. The sea was rocking, and shaken with gathering wrath. Upon its surface sate mighty mists, which grouped themselves into arches and long cathedral aisles. Down one of these, with the fiery pace of a quarrel from a cross-bow, ran a frigate right athwart our course.' Are they mad?' some voice exclaimed from our deck.' Are they blind? Do they woo their ruin?' But in a moment, as she was close upon us, some impulse of a heady current or sudden vortex gave a wheeling bias to her course, and off she forged without a shock. As she ran past us, high aloft amongst the shrouds stood the lady of the pinnace. The deeps opened ahead in malice to receive her, towering surges of foam ran after her, the billows were fierce to catch her. But far away she was borne into desert spaces of the sea: whilst still by sight I followed her, as she ran before the howling gale, chased by angry sea-birds and by maddening billows; still I saw her, as at the moment when she ran past us, amongst the shrouds, with her white draperies streaming before the wind. There she stood with hair dishevelled, one hand clutched amongst the tackling—rising, sinking, fluttering, trembling, praying - there for leagues I saw her as she stood, raising at intervals one hand to heaven, amidst the fiery crests of the pursuing waves and the raving of the storm; until at last, upon a sound from afar of malicious laughter and mockery, all was hidden for ever in driving showers; and afterwards, but when I know not, and how I know not.

3

Sweet funeral bells from some incalculable distance, wailing over the dead that die before the dawn, awakened me as I slept in a boat moored to some familiar shore. The morning twilight even then was breaking; and, by the dusky revelations which it spread, I saw a girl adorned with a garland of white roses about her head for some great festival, running along the solitary strand with extremity of haste. Her running was the running of panic; and often she looked back as to some dreadful enemy in the rear. But when I leaped ashore, and followed on her steps to warn her of a peril in front, alas! from me she fled as from another peril; and vainly I shouted to her of quicksands that lay ahead. Faster and faster she ran; round a promontory of rocks she wheeled out of sight; in an instant I also wheeled round it, but only to see the treacherous sands gathering above her head. Already her person was buried; only the fair young head and the diadem of white roses around it were still visible to the pitying heavens; and, last of all, was visible one marble arm. I saw by the early twilight this fair young head, as it was sinking down to darkness - saw this marble arm, as it rose above her head and her treacherous grave, tossing, faultering, rising, clutching as at some false deceiving hand stretched out from the clouds — saw this marble arm uttering her dying hope, and then her dying despair. The head, the diadem, the arm,—these all had sunk; at last over these also the cruel quicksand had closed; and no memorial of the fair young girl remained on earth, except my own solitary tears, and the funeral bells from the desert seas, that, rising again more softly, sang a requiem over the grave of the buried child, and over her blighted dawn.

I sate, and wept in secret the tears that men have ever given to the memory of those that died before the dawn, and by the treachery of earth, our mother. But the tears and funeral bells were hushed suddenly by a shout as of many nations, and by a roar as from some great king's artillery advancing rapidly along the valleys, and heard afar by its

echoes among the mountains.' Hush!' I said, as I bent my ear earthwards to listen-
'hush!—this either is the very anarchy of strife, or else'-and then I listened more
profoundly, and said as I raised my head-' or else, oh heavens! it is *victory* that swallows
up all strife.'

4

Immediately, in trance, I was carried over land and sea to some distant kingdom, and
placed upon a triumphal car, amongst companions crowned with laurel. The darkness of
gathering midnight, brooding over all the land, hid from us the mighty crowds that were
weaving restlessly about our carriage as a centre — we heard them, but we saw them not.
Tidings had arrived, within an hour, of a grandeur that measured itself against centuries;
too full of pathos they were, too full of joy that acknowledged no fountain but God, to
utter themselves by other language than by tears, by restless anthems, by reverberations
rising from every choir, of the *Gloria in excelsis*. These tidings we that sate upon the
laurelled car had it for our privilege to publish amongst all nations. And already, by signs
audible through the darkness, by snortings and tramplings, our angry horses, that knew no
fear of fleshly weariness, upbraided us with delay. Wherefore *was* it that we delayed? We
waited for a secret word, that should bear witness to the hope of nations, as now
accomplished for ever. At midnight the secret word arrived; which word was—Waterloo
and Recovered Christendom! The dreadful word shone by its own light; before us it went;
high above our leaders' heads it rode and spread a golden light over the paths which we
traversed. Every city, at the presence of the secret word, threw open its gates to receive
us. The rivers were silent as we crossed. All the infinite forests, as we ran along their
margins, shivered in homage to the secret word. And the darkness comprehended it.

Two hours after midnight we reached a mighty minster. Its gates, which rose to the
clouds, were closed. But when the dreadful word, that rode before us, reached them with
its golden light, silently they moved back upon their hinges; and at a flying gallop our
equipage entered the grand aisle of the cathedral. Headlong was our pace; and at every
altar, in the little chapels and oratories to the right hand and left of our course, the lamps,
dying or sickening, kindled anew in sympathy with the secret word that was flying past.
Forty leagues we might have run in the cathedral, and as yet no strength of morning light
had reached us, when we saw before us the aerial galleries of the organ and the choir.
Every pinnacle of the fretwork, every station of advantage amongst the traceries, was
crested by white-robed choristers, that sang deliverance; that wept no more tears, as once
their fathers had wept; but at intervals that sang together to the generations, saying-

"Chant the deliverer's praise in every tongue,"

and receiving answers from afar,

—"such as once in heaven and earth were sung."

And of their chanting was no end; of our headlong pace was neither pause nor remission.

Thus, as we ran like torrents—thus, as we swept with bridal rapture over the Campo
Santo [47] of the cathedral graves— suddenly we became aware of a vast necropolis
rising upon the far-off horizon—a city of sepulchres, built within the saintly cathedral for
the warrior dead that rested from their feuds on earth. Of purple granite was the

necropolis; yet, in the first minute, it lay like a purple stain upon the horizon—so mighty was the distance. In the second minute it trembled through many changes, growing into terraces and towers of wondrous altitude, so mighty was the pace. In the third minute already, with our dreadful gallop, we were entering its suburbs. Vast sarcophagi rose on every side, having towers and turrets that, upon the limits of the central aisle, strode forward with haughty intrusion, that ran back with mighty shadows into answering recesses. Every sarcophagus showed many bas-reliefs,—bas-reliefs of battles— bas-reliefs of battle-fields; of battles from forgotten ages of battles from yesterday—of battle-fields that, long since, nature had healed and reconciled to herself with the sweet oblivion of flowers- of battle-fields that were yet angry and crimson with carnage. Where the terraces ran, there did we run; where the towers curved, there did we curve. With the flight of swallows our horses swept round every angle. Like rivers in flood, wheeling round headlands; like hurricanes that side into the secrets of forests; faster than ever light unwove the mazes of darkness, our flying equipage carried earthly passions- kindled warrior instincts—amongst the dust that lay around us; dust oftentimes of our noble fathers that had slept in God from Créci to Trafalgar. And now had we reached the last sarcophagus, now were we abreast of the last bas-relief, already had we recovered the arrow-like flight of the illimitable central aisle, when coming up this aisle to meet us we beheld a female infant that rode in a carriage as frail as flowers. The mists, which went before her, hid the fawns that drew her, but could not hide the shells and tropic flowers with which she played—but could not hide the lovely smiles by which she uttered her trust in the mighty cathedral, and in the cherubim that looked down upon her from the topmost shafts of its pillars. Face to face she was meeting us; face to face she rode, as if danger there were none.' Oh, baby!' I exclaimed, shalt thou be the ransom for Waterloo? Must we, that carry tidings of great joy to every people, be messengers of ruin to thee?' In horror I rose at the thought; but then also, in horror at the thought, rose one that was sculptured on the bas-relief- a dying trumpeter. Solemnly from the field of battle he rose to his feet; and, unslinging his stony trumpet, carried it, in his dying anguish, to his stony lips—sounding once, and yet once again; proclamation that, in *thy* ears, oh baby! must have spoken from the battlements of death. Immediately deep shadows fell between us, and aboriginal silence. The choir had ceased to sing. The hoofs of our horses, the rattling of our harness, alarmed the graves no more. By horror the bas-relief had been unlocked into life. By horror we, that were so full of life, we men and our horses, with their fiery fore-legs rising in mid air to their everlasting gallop, were frozen to a bas-relief. Then a third time the trumpet sounded; the seals were taken off all pulses; life, and the frenzy of life, tore into their channels again; again the choir burst forth in sunny grandeur, as from the muffling of storms and darkness; again the thunderings of our horses carried temptation into the graves. One cry burst from our lips as the clouds, drawing off from the aisle, showed it empty before us -' Whither has the infant fled? is the young child caught up to God?' Lo! afar off, in a vast recess, rose three mighty windows to the clouds: and on a level with their summits, at height insuperable to man, rose an altar of purest alabaster. On its eastern face was trembling a crimson glory. Whence came *that*? Was it from the reddening dawn that now streamed *through* the windows? Was it from the crimson robes of the martyrs that were painted on the windows? Was it from the bloody bas-reliefs of earth? Whencesoever it were—there, within that crimson radiance, suddenly appeared a female head, and then a female figure. It was the child- now grown up to woman's height. Clinging to the horns of the altar, there she stood—sinking, rising, trembling, fainting,—raving, despairing; and behind the volume of incense that, night and day, streamed upwards from the altar, was seen the fiery font, and dimly was descried the outline of the dreadful being that should baptize her with the baptism of death. But by her side was kneeling her better angel, that hid his face with wings; that wept and pleaded for her; that prayed when *she* could *not*; that fought with heaven by tears for *her* deliverance; which also, as he raised his immortal countenance from his wings, I saw, by the glory in his eye, that he had won at last.

5

Then rose the agitation, spreading through the infinite cathedral, to its agony; then was completed the passion of the mighty fugue. The golden tubes of the organ, which as yet had but sobbed and muttered at intervals—gleaming amongst clouds and surges of incense—threw up, as from fountains unfathomable, columns of heart-shattering music. Choir and antichoir were filling fast with unknown voices. Thou also, Dying Trumpeter!—with thy love that was victorious, and thy anguish that was finishing, didst enter the tumult: trumpet and echo—farewell love, and farewell anguish—rang, through the dreadful *sanctus*. We, that spread flight before us, heard the tumult, as of flight, mustering behind us. In fear we looked round for the unknown steps that, in flight or in pursuit, were gathering upon our own. Who were these that followed? The faces, which no man could count whence were *they*? 'Oh, darkness of the grave!' I exclaimed, 'that from the crimson altar and from the fiery font wert visited with secret light—that wert searched by the indulgence in the angel's eye—were these indeed thy children.? Pomps of life, that, from the burials of centuries, rose again to the voice of perfect joy, could it be ye that had wrapped me in the reflux of panic?' What ailed me, that I should fear when the triumphs of earth were advancing? Ah! Pariah heart within me, that couldst never hear the sound of joy without sullen whispers of treachery in ambush; that, from six years old, didst never hear the promise of perfect love, without seeing aloft amongst the stars fingers as of a man's hand, writing the secret legend -'*Ashes to ashes, dust to dust*!' wherefore shouldst *thou* not fear, though all men should rejoice? Lo! as I looked back for seventy leagues through the mighty cathedral, and. saw the quick and the dead that sang together to God, together that sang to the generations of man—ah! raving, as of torrents that opened on every side: trepidation, as of female and infant steps that fled—ah! rushing, as of wings that chase! But I heard a voice from heaven, which said -'Let there be no reflux of panic—let there be no more fear, and no more sudden death! Cover them with joy as the tides cover the shore!' *That* heard the children of the choir, *that* heard the children of the grave. All the hosts of jubilation made ready to move. Like armies that ride in pursuit, they moved with one step. Us, that, with laurelled heads, were passing from the cathedral through its eastern gates, they overtook, and, as with a garment, they wrapped us round with thunders that overpowered our own. As brothers we moved together; to the skies we rose —to the dawn that advanced-to the stars that fled; rendering thanks to God in the highest—that, having hid his face through one generation behind thick clouds of War, once again was ascending—was ascending from Waterloo—in the visions of Peace: rendering thanks for thee, young girl whom having overshadowed with his ineffable passion of death—suddenly did God relent; suffered thy angel to turn aside his arm; and even in thee, sister unknown! shown to me for a moment only to be hidden for ever, found an occasion to glorify his goodness. A thousand times, amongst the phantoms of sleep, has he shown thee to me, standing before the golden dawn, and ready to enter its gates—with the dreadful word going before thee—with the armies of the grave behind thee; shown thee to me, sinking, rising, fluttering, fainting, but then suddenly reconciled, adoring: a thousand times has he followed thee in the worlds of sleep—through storms; through desert seas; through the darkness of quicksands; through fugues and the persecution of fugues; through dreams, and the dreadful resurrections that are in dreams—only that at the last, with one motion of his victorious arm, he might record and emblazon the endless resurrections of his love!

THE END

Lightning Source UK Ltd.
Milton Keynes UK
UKOW02f0828240915

259179UK00003B/135/P